30 DEVOTIONALS

GOD'S PLAN *for* YOUR LIFE
OVERCOMING FINANCIAL CHALLENGES

Standard & Poor's 500-stock ind

Yield Curve

D1437548

BIBLICAL PRINCIPLES TO GUIDE YOU
IN YOUR JOURNEY THROUGH TIGHT TIMES

FAMILY
Christian Stores·

Scripture quotations are taken from:

The Holy Bible, King James Version (KJV)

The Holy Bible, New International Version (NIV) Copyright © 1973, 1978, 1984, by International Bible Society. Used by permission of Zondervan Publishing House. All rights reserved.

The Holy Bible, New King James Version (NKJV) Copyright © 1982 by Thomas Nelson, Inc. Used by permission.

Holy Bible, New Living Translation, (NLT) copyright © 1996. Used by permission of Tyndale House Publishers, Inc., Wheaton, Illinois 60189. All rights reserved.

The Message (MSG)- This edition issued by contractual arrangement with NavPress, a division of The Navigators, U.S.A. Originally published by NavPress in English as THE MESSAGE: The Bible in Contemporary Language copyright 2002-2003 by Eugene Peterson. All rights reserved.

New Century Version®. (NCV) Copyright © 1987, 1988, 1991 by Word Publishing, a division of Thomas Nelson, Inc. All rights reserved. Used by permission.

The New American Standard Bible®, (NASB) Copyright © 1960, 1962, 1963, 1968, 1971, 1972, 1973, 1975, 1977, 1995 by The Lockman Foundation. Used by permission.

The Holman Christian Standard Bible™ (HCSB) Copyright © 1999, 2000, 2001 by Holman Bible Publishers. Used by permission.

Cover Design & Page Layout by Bart Dawson

ISBN 978-1-160587-055-7

Printed in the United States of America

30 DEVOTIONALS

GOD'S PLAN *for* YOUR LIFE
OVERCOMING FINANCIAL CHALLENGES

Standard & Poor's 500-stock ind

350

Yield Curve

BIBLICAL PRINCIPLES TO GUIDE YOU IN YOUR JOURNEY THROUGH TIGHT TIMES

TABLE OF CONTENTS

INTRODUCTION

"We know that all things work together for the good of those who love God: those who are called according to His purpose."

Romans 8:28 HCSB

God's Word promises that all things work together for the good of those who love Him. Yet sometimes we encounter challenges that seem so troubling, and so perplexing, that we cannot understand how these events might be a part of God's plan for our lives. Many of these challenges have to do with money.

When we experience tough financial times, we may honestly wonder if recovery is possible. But with God, all things are possible. After all, the Christian faith is a healing faith. And God has made promises to all of us, promises that He will certainly keep.

This book is intended to assist you as you reorganize your finances to consider God's instructions for your life and your finances. As such, this text is divided into 30 chapters, one for each day of the month. During the next 30 days, please try this experiment: read at least one chapter each day. If you're already committed to a daily time of worship, this book will enrich that experience. If you are not, the simple act of giving God a few minutes each morning will help you establish proper priorities for the coming day.

So, for the next 30 days, read one chapter a day and take the ideas in that chapter to heart. Then, apply those lessons to the everyday realities of managing your money and your life. When you weave God's message into the fabric of your day, you'll quickly discover that God's Word has the power to change everything, including you.

Tough financial times are temporary, but God's promises are eternal. Trust Him with your money and your life. When you do, He will bless you and keep you today, tomorrow, and forever.

Day 1

There Are No Problems That You and God, Working Together, Can't Handle

"For I know the plans I have for you," declares the Lord,
"plans to prosper you and not to harm you, plans to give you
hope and a future. Then you will call upon me and come
and pray to me, and I will listen to you."

Jeremiah 29:11-12 NIV

The Focus for Today

Money is a training ground for God to develop—
and for us to discover—our trustworthiness.

Larry Burkett

If you're experiencing financial headaches, please don't feel like the Lone Ranger! Almost everyone experiences financial pressures from time to time, and so, perhaps, will you.

Winston Churchill once observed, "Success is going from failure to failure without loss of enthusiasm." What was good for Churchill is also good for you, too. As you live and learn about life, you should expect to make mistakes—and a few financial blunders, too—but you should not allow those missteps to rob you of the enthusiasm you need to fulfill God's plan for your life.

The fact that you encounter economic hardship is not nearly so important as the way you choose to deal with it. When tough times arrive, you have a clear choice: you can begin the difficult work of tackling your troubles . . . or not. When you summon the courage to look Old Man Trouble squarely in the eye, he usually blinks. But, if you refuse to address your problems, even the smallest annoyances have a way of growing into king-sized catastrophes.

Psalm 145 promises, "The Lord is near to all who call on him, to all who call on him in truth. He fulfills the desires of those who fear him; he hears their cry and saves them" (v. 18-20 NIV). And the words of Jesus offer us comfort: "These things I have spoken to you, that in Me you may have peace. In the world you will have tribulation; but be of good cheer, I have overcome the world" (John 16:33 NKJV).

As believers, we know that God loves us and that He will protect us. In times of hardship, He will comfort us; in times of need, He will give us strength. When we are troubled, or weak, or sorrowful, God is always with us. We must build our lives on the rock that cannot be shaken: we must trust in God. And then, we must get on with the hard work of tackling our problems . . . because if we don't, who will? Or should?

GOD'S PLAN AND YOUR FINANCIAL CHALLENGES

Why does God allow us to endure tough times? After all, since we trust that God is all-powerful, and since we trust that His hand shapes our lives, why doesn't He simply rescue us—and our loved ones—from all hardship and pain?

God's Word teaches us again and again that He loves us and wants the best for us. And the Bible also teaches us that God is ever-present and always watchful. So why, we wonder, if God is really so concerned with every detail of our lives, does He permit us to make mistakes and to endure emotions like sadness, shame, or fear? And why does He allow troubles and tribulations to invade the lives of good people? These questions perplex us, especially when times are tough.

On occasion, all of us face adversity, and throughout

life, we all must endure life-changing personal losses that leave us breathless. When we pass through the dark valleys of life, we often ask, "Why me?" Sometimes, of course, the answer is obvious—sometimes we make mistakes, and we must pay for them. But on other occasions, when we have done nothing wrong, we wonder why God allows us to suffer.

Even when we cannot understand God's plans, we must trust them. And even when we are impatient for our situations to improve, we must trust God's timing. If we seek to live in accordance with His plan for our lives, we must continue to study His Word (in good times and bad), and we must be watchful for His signs, knowing that in time, He will lead us through the valleys, onward to the mountaintop.

So if you're enduring tough economic times, don't give up and don't give in. God still has glorious plans for you. So keep your eyes and ears open . . . as well as your heart.

TODAY'S TIP FOR HANDLING TOUGH TIMES

God has the power to repair anything, including your financial difficulties. But He won't do it alone; He requires your cooperation, your obedience, your willingness to work hard, and your willingness to make smart decisions.

MORE FROM GOD'S WORD ABOUT
GOD'S PROTECTION

When you pass through the waters, I will be with you; and through the rivers, they shall not overflow you. When you walk through the fire, you shall not be burned, nor shall the flame scorch you. For I am the Lord your God, The Holy One of Israel, your Savior.

Isaiah 43:2-3 NKJV

We also have joy with our troubles, because we know that these troubles produce patience. And patience produces character, and character produces hope.

Romans 5:3-4 NCV

The LORD also will be a stronghold for the oppressed, a stronghold in times of trouble.

Psalm 9:9 NASB

Don't fret or worry, Instead of worrying, pray. Let petitions and praises shape your worries into prayers, letting God know your concerns. Before you know it, a sense of God's wholeness, everything coming together for good, will come and settle you down. It's wonderful what happens when Christ displaces worry at the center of your life.

Philippians 4:6-7 MSG

MORE POWERFUL IDEAS ABOUT ADVERSITY

When problems threaten to engulf us, we must do what believers have always done, turn to the Lord for encouragement and solace. As Psalm 46:1 states, "God is our refuge and strength, an ever-present help in trouble."

Shirley Dobson

A faith that hasn't been tested can't be trusted.

Adrian Rogers

It's a good thing to have all the props pulled out from under us occasionally. It gives us some sense of what rock is under our feet, and what is sand. It stops us from taking anything for granted.

Madeleine L'Engle

Don't let circumstances distress you. Rather, look for the will of God for your life to be revealed in and through those circumstances.

Billy Graham

Each problem is a God-appointed instructor.

Charles Swindoll

Like Paul, we may bear thorns
so that we can discover
God's perfect sufficiency.

—

Beth Moore

QUESTIONS TO CONSIDER

Am I really seeking God's will for my life, or am I just going through the motions?

_____

_____

Since I believe that God has a plan for my life, do I believe that He can help me overcome my financial challenges and then bring something good out of my hardships?

_____

_____

Do I regularly ask God to reveal His plans to me, and when I pray, do I listen carefully for His response?

_____

_____

A PRAYER FOR TODAY

Dear Lord, You have a plan for me and a plan for this world. Let me trust Your will, and let me discover Your plan for my life so that I can become the person You want me to become. Amen

Day 2

PUT GOD FIRST

You shall have no other gods before Me.

Exodus 20:3 NKJV

THE FOCUS FOR TODAY

Jesus Christ is the first and last, author and finisher,
beginning and end, alpha and omega, and by Him all
other things hold together. He must be first or nothing.
God never comes next!

Vance Havner

As you consider ways to achieve financial security, it's wise to place first things first, starting with God. Is God your top priority? Have you decided to give His Son your heart, your soul, your talents, and your time? Or are you in the habit of giving God little more than a few hours on Sunday mornings? The answer to these questions will determine how you prioritize your time and how you prioritize your life.

Whether you're at work, at home, or someplace in between, you're engaged in worship. In fact, all of mankind is engaged in worship—of one sort or another. Some people choose to worship God and, as a result, reap the joy that He intends for His children. Others distance themselves from God by worshiping such things as earthly possessions or personal gratification . . . and when they do so, they suffer.

In the book of Exodus, God warns that we should place no gods before Him. Yet all too often, we place our Lord in second, third, or fourth place as we worship the gods of pride, greed, power, or lust. When we place our desires for material possessions above our love for God—or when we yield to the countless temptations that surround us—we find ourselves engaged in a struggle that is similar to the one Jesus faced when He was tempted by Satan. In the wilderness, Satan offered Jesus earthly power and unimaginable riches, but Jesus turned Satan away and chose instead to worship God. We must do likewise by putting God first and worshiping only Him.

Is God in charge of your heart, your mind, your career, and your finances? Make certain that the honest answer to this question is a resounding yes. God must come first. Always first.

WHEN YOUR FAITH IS TESTED

Life is a tapestry of good days and difficult days, with good days predominating. During the good days, we are tempted to take our blessings for granted (a temptation that we must resist with all our might). But, during life's difficult days, we discover precisely what we're made of. And more importantly, we discover what our faith is made of.

Has your faith been put to the test yet? If so, then you know that with God's help, you can endure life's darker days. But if you have not yet faced the inevitable trials and tragedies of life here on earth, don't worry: you will. And when your faith is put to the test, rest assured that God is perfectly willing—and always ready—to give you strength for the struggle.

TODAY'S TIP FOR HANDLING TOUGH TIMES

Seek spiritual health first and financial health second. To do otherwise is risk God's disapproval.

MORE FROM GOD'S WORD ABOUT PUTTING GOD FIRST

Be still, and know that I am God.

Psalm 46:10 NKJV

The Devil said to Him, "I will give You their splendor and all this authority, because it has been given over to me, and I can give it to anyone I want. If You, then, will worship me, all will be Yours." And Jesus answered him, "It is written: You shall worship the Lord your God, and Him alone you shall serve."

Luke 4:6-8 HCSB

Another also said, "I will follow You, Lord, but first let me go and say good-bye to those at my house." But Jesus said to him, "No one who puts his hand to the plow and looks back is fit for the kingdom of God."

Luke 9:61-62 HCSB

MORE POWERFUL IDEAS ABOUT
GOD'S ABILITY TO GUIDE AND PROTECT

If God has the power to create and sustain the universe, He is more than able to sustain your marriage and your ministry, your faith and your finances, your hope and your health.

Anne Graham Lotz

One with God is a majority.

Billy Graham

When all else is gone, God is still left. Nothing changes Him.

Hannah Whitall Smith

It is when we come to the Lord in our nothingness, our powerlessness and our helplessness that He then enables us to love in a way which, without Him, would be absolutely impossible.

Elisabeth Elliot

A man's spiritual health is exactly proportional to his love for God.

C. S. Lewis

QUESTIONS TO CONSIDER

To determine who is in charge of your finances, answer the following True or False questions:

True or False God is my ultimate financial advisor. I will trust Him with everything I have.

True or False I understand the importance of being a careful steward of the money that God has entrusted to my care.

True or False I will be generous with my tithes and offerings because I understand that everything I have ultimately belongs to God.

True or False When I have a question about my finances, I'm willing to pray about it.

A PRAYER FOR TODAY

Dear Lord, You are the rock upon which I will build my life. You have given me so much, and I am thankful. I give thanks for Your gifts— and I will share them today and every day. Amen

Day 3

GOD HAS A PLAN FOR YOUR FINANCES, AND IT'S SIMPLER THAN YOU THINK

I will instruct you and show you the way to go;
with My eye on you, I will give counsel.

Psalm 32:8 HCSB

THE FOCUS FOR TODAY

God never leads us astray.
He knows exactly where He's taking us.
Our job is to obey.

Charles Swindoll

Countless books have been written about money—how to make it and how to keep it. But if you're a Christian, you probably already own at least one copy—and probably several copies—of the world's foremost guide to financial security. That book is the Holy Bible. God's Word is not only a roadmap to eternal life, but it is also an indispensable guidebook for life here on earth. As such, the Bible has much to say about your life, your faith, and your finances.

God's Word reminds us again and again that our Creator expects us to lead disciplined lives. God doesn't reward laziness, misbehavior, or apathy. To the contrary, He expects believers to behave with dignity and discipline not as the world tempts us. We live in a world in which leisure is glorified and indifference is often glamorized. But God has other plans. He did not create us for lives of mediocrity; He created us for far greater things.

Life's greatest rewards seldom fall into our laps; to the contrary, our greatest accomplishments (including our financial accomplishments) usually require lots of work, a heaping helping of common sense, and a double dose of self-discipline—which is perfectly fine with God. After all, He knows that we're up to the task.

God's Word can help you organize your financial affairs in such a way that you have less need to worry and more time to celebrate. If that sounds appealing, keep reading God's book and apply it to every aspect of your life, including the way that you handle money. When you do, God will smile upon you and your finances.

TRUST HIS PLAN

Sometimes, waiting faithfully for God's plan to unfold is more important than understanding God's plan. Ruth Bell Graham once said, "When I am dealing with an all-powerful, all-knowing God, I, as a mere mortal, must offer my petitions not only with persistence, but also with patience. Someday I'll know why." So even when you can't understand God's plans, you must trust Him and never lose faith!

TODAY'S TIP FOR HANDLING TOUGH TIMES

The road to financial freedom is well-marked, and the most important signposts are found in God's Word. Thankfully, God's financial guidance isn't very complicated. He wants us to work diligently, to spend carefully, to save consistently, and to avoid the quicksand of debt. But what if you're already deeply in debt? Well, digging yourself out of the money pit may be hard, even painful at times. But with God as your partner, you can do it.

MORE FROM GOD'S WORD ABOUT
GOD'S INSTRUCTION

In all your ways acknowledge Him, and He shall direct your paths.

Proverbs 3:6 NKJV

Yet Lord, You are our Father; we are the clay, and You are our potter; we all are the work of Your hands.

Isaiah 64:8 HCSB

Lord, You are my lamp; the Lord illuminates my darkness.

2 Samuel 22:29 HCSB

The true children of God are those who let God's Spirit lead them.

Romans 8:14 NCV

Teach me Your way, Lord, and I will live by Your truth. Give me an undivided mind to fear Your name.

Psalm 86:11 HCSB

MORE POWERFUL IDEAS ABOUT GOD'S GUIDANCE

Enjoy the adventure of receiving God guidance. Taste it, revel in it, appreciate the fact that the journey is often a lot more exciting than arriving at the destination.

Bill Hybels

Christians cannot experience peace in the area of finances until they have surrendered total control of this area to God and accepted their position as stewards.

Larry Burkett

Are you serious about wanting God's guidance to become a personal reality in your life? The first step is to tell God that you know you can't manage your own life; that you need his help.

Catherine Marshall

If we want to hear God's voice, we must surrender our minds and hearts to Him.

Billy Graham

We all go through pain and sorrow, but the presence of God, like a warm, comforting blanket, can shield us and protect us, and allow the deep inner joy to surface, even in the most devastating circumstances.

Barbara Johnson

QUESTIONS TO CONSIDER

Am I willing to devote the time to be with God?

_____

_____

Am I willing to be still and listen to God, or do I think that I already have all the answers I need?

_____

_____

Am I willing to focus my thoughts and prayers on the things that God wants me to do today, this year, and in years to come?

_____

_____

A PRAYER FOR TODAY

Dear Lord, today I come to You seeking guidance.
I will trust You to show me the path that I should take,
and I will strive, as best I can, to follow in the footsteps
of Your Son. Amen.

Day 4

OVERCOMING DENIAL:
IF YOU'RE UNDERWATER,
YOUR FIRST JOB IS
TO START SWIMMING
TO THE SURFACE

Discretion is a life-giving fountain to those who possess it,
but discipline is wasted on fools.
Proverbs 16:22 NLT

THE FOCUS FOR TODAY

The single most important element in any human
relationship is honesty—with oneself,
with God, and with others.
Catherine Marshall

Before you can start tackling financial challenges, you must admit that you have financial challenges. But admitting that you're in trouble can be hard. After all, making the admission (to other people or to yourself) that you have not managed money wisely can be embarrassing. Besides, the world continues to pump out a vast array of products and services that you'd like to buy if you could afford them. And to make matters worse, the popular media is brimming with messages that it's better to borrow and buy than to save. So, until you "hit the wall" financially, you'll be tempted to deny that you have a money problem. But denial can be dangerous to your health, financial or otherwise.

Denial is insidious. It has a way of sneaking up on all of us, allowing us to overlook our own shortcomings. But if we deny our shortcomings, we allow them to flourish. And if we allow unwise behaviors to become habits, we invite hardships into our own lives and into the lives of our loved ones.

Unless you were blindsided by medical expenses or some other unforeseeable financial tidal wave that was totally outside your control, you probably still have lots to learn about making, managing, and saving money—and that's nothing to be ashamed of. Your challenge, of course is to face up to your past mistakes and learn from them, starting now.

There's none so blind as those who will not see.

—

Matthew Henry

TODAY'S TIP FOR HANDLING TOUGH TIMES

Be proactive. Call your lender before your lender calls you. And keep calling until you reach a decision-maker who can help you make payment arrangements you can afford.

MORE FROM GOD'S WORD ABOUT FACING REALITY

Buy—and do not sell—truth, wisdom, instruction, and understanding.

Proverbs 23:23 HCSB

I have no greater joy than this, to hear of my children walking in the truth.

3 John 1:4 NASB

For everyone who practices wicked things hates the light and avoids it, so that his deeds may not be exposed. But anyone who lives by the truth comes to the light, so that his works may be shown to be accomplished by God.

John 3:20-21 HCSB

We justify our actions by appearances; God examines our motives.

Proverbs 21:2 MSG

You will know the truth, and the truth will set you free.

John 8:32 HCSB

MORE POWERFUL IDEAS ABOUT FACING UP TO UNPLEASANT REALITIES, WHETHER THEY BE FINANCIAL OR OTHERWISE

Honesty simply asks if we are open, willing, and able to acknowledge this truth. Honesty brings an end to pretense through a candid acknowledgment of our fragile humanity.

Brennan Manning

Man prefers to believe what he prefers to be true.

Francis Bacon

What I like about experience is that it is such an honest thing. You may take any number of wrong turnings; but keep your eyes open and you will not be allowed to go very far before the warning signs appear. You may have deceived yourself, but experience is not trying to deceive you. The universe rings true wherever you fairly test it.

C. S. Lewis

Let us take things as we find them: let us not attempt to distort them into what they are not. We cannot make facts. All our wishing cannot change them. We must use them.

John Henry Cardinal Newman

QUESTIONS TO CONSIDER

In the past, What financial problems have I overlooked that, in retrospect, now seem obvious?

_____

_____

_____

_____

_____

_____

What financial realities do I need to face today?

_____

_____

_____

_____

_____

_____

_____

A PRAYER FOR TODAY

_Dear Lord, help me see the truth, and help me respond
to the things that I see with determination,
wisdom, and courage. Amen_

Day 5

THE POWER OF A PLAN

The plans of the diligent certainly lead to profit,
but anyone who is reckless only becomes poor.
Proverbs 21:5 HCSB

THE FOCUS FOR TODAY

Let our advance worrying become
advance thinking and planning.
Winston Churchill

It's easier to overcome financial challenges if you have a clear plan. A written plan. A plan that you and your family can understand. A plan that you and your family can live with. So, here's a word to the wise: start with a plan that makes sense to you and to God. An intelligent financial plan is an integral part of your long-term financial security. But planning is not enough; you must also be willing to stick with the plan you make. In other words, financial security requires intelligent planning and disciplined implementation.

Your financial plan is not merely a collection of numbers on a page; it is, more importantly, a reflection of your faith and your values. And, if you seek God's blessings, you will establish your plans in accordance with His commandments.

You've probably heard the song "My Way" (it was Frank Sinatra's theme song, and Elvis sang it, too). "My Way" is a perfectly good tune, but it's not a perfect guide for life here on earth. If you're looking for life's perfect prescription—if you're looking for joy, peace, abundance, and eternal life—you'd better forget about doing things your way and start doing things God's way.

God has plans for your life. Big plans. But He won't force you to obey His commandments; to the contrary, He has given you free will, the ability to make choices on your own. With the freedom to choose comes the responsibility of living with the consequences of the choices you make.

The most important decision of your life is, of course, your commitment to accept Jesus Christ as your personal Lord and Savior. And once your eternal destiny is secured, you will undoubtedly ask yourself the question "What now, Lord?" And when you ask that question, you may rest assured that part of God's plan for your life includes a disciplined approach to your finances.

As a Christian, your financial plan should be an outgrowth of your commitment to obey God's Holy Word. As such, you must gladly offer God the tithe to which He is entitled (Malachi 3:10). If you intend for your tithe to be substantial, you should plan to maximize your income by continuing to improve your skills (thus improving your earning potential). Additionally, your financial plan should include provisions for insurance (life, health, auto, and home, at a minimum). And of course, your financial plan should also include provisions for a reasonable cash cushion (think of it as a "rainy day" fund) as well as a sensible retirement strategy.

If all this planning seems like a considerable amount of work, take a moment to consider the alternative: Without a plan to guide you, you'll be far more likely to squander your resources, including a most precious resource: your time. So, if you haven't already done so, take this opportunity to formulate a written financial plan for you and your family. And then, when you've committed yourself to a common-sense financial strategy, you're ready to create the indispensable tool for implementing your plan; that tool is your household budget, which is the subject of day 8 on page 53.

TODAY'S TIP FOR HANDLING TOUGH TIMES

It may take a few hours to commit your financial plans to paper, but it's most certainly worth the time and effort. Putting your plan down in black and white helps you clarify your thoughts, focus your energies, and measure your results.

MORE FROM GOD'S WORD ABOUT PLANNING

Commit your work to the LORD, and then your plans will succeed.

Proverbs 16:3 NLT

Let your eyes look forward; fix your gaze straight ahead.

Proverbs 4:25 HCSB

But the noble man makes noble plans, and by noble deeds he stands.

Isaiah 32:8 NIV

MORE POWERFUL IDEAS ABOUT PLANNING

Plan your work. Without a system, you'll feel swamped.

Norman Vincent Peale

God has a plan for your life . . . do you?

Jim Gallery

The only way you can experience abundant life is to surrender your plans to Him.

Charles Stanley

Allow your dreams a place in your prayers and plans. God-given dreams can help you move into the future He is preparing for you.

Barbara Johnson

Think ahead—it's the best way of making sure you don't get left behind.

Criswell Freeman

Plan ahead—it wasn't raining when Noah built the ark.

Anonymous

QUESTIONS TO CONSIDER

What are the benefits of investing the time and energy required to create a clear budget and a solid financial plan?

_____

_____

_____

_____

_____

_____

And what are the rewards if I live by that plan?

_____

_____

_____

_____

_____

A PRAYER FOR TODAY

_Dear Lord, help me accept the past, help me enjoy
the present, and help me plan for the future.
While I am doing these things, help me to trust You
more and more . . . this day and every day. Amen_

Day 6

FINANCIAL RECOVERY CAN ALSO BE A SPIRITUAL JOURNEY

*So don't lose a minute in building on what you've been given,
complementing your basic faith with good character, spiritual
understanding, alert discipline, passionate patience, reverent
wonder, warm friendliness, and generous love,
each dimension fitting into and developing the others.*
2 Peter 1:5-7 MSG

THE FOCUS FOR TODAY

Adversity is not simply a tool. It is God's most effective
tool for the advancement of our spiritual lives.
The circumstances and events that we see as setbacks are
oftentimes the very things that launch us into periods of
intense spiritual growth. Once we begin to understand
this, and accept it as a spiritual fact of life,
adversity becomes easier to bear.

Charles Stanley

The path to spiritual maturity unfolds day by day, through good times and hard times. Each day offers the opportunity to worship God, to ignore God, or to rebel against God. When we worship Him with our prayers, our words, our thoughts, and our actions, we are blessed by the richness of our relationship with the Father. But if we ignore God altogether or intentionally rebel against His commandments, we rob ourselves of His blessings.

Since many of life's most important lessons are painful to learn, times of hardship can also be times of growth. So if you're enduring tough times, you can be sure that God has things He wants you to learn. Your job is to be teachable.

In those quiet moments when you open your heart to the Father, He will give you direction, hope, perspective, and courage. And, the appropriate moment to accept those spiritual gifts is always the present one.

Has your financial life been turned upside down? Are you enduring tough times that have left your head spinning? Are you worried, or discouraged, or both? If so, you can be certain that God has important lessons to teach you. So ask yourself this: What lesson is God trying to teach me today? And then go about the business of learning it.

OLD MAN TROUBLE HAS LESSONS TO TEACH

The next time Old Man Trouble knocks on your door, remember that he has lessons to teach. So turn away Mr. Trouble as quickly as you can, but as you're doing so, don't forget to learn his lessons. And remember: the trouble with trouble isn't just the trouble it causes; it's also the trouble we cause ourselves if we ignore the things that trouble has to teach. Got that? Then please don't forget it!

TODAY'S TIP FOR HANDLING TOUGH TIMES

The times that test our souls can also be times of intense personal growth. Elisabeth Elliot observed, "I am not a theologian or a scholar, but I am very aware of the fact that pain is necessary to all of us. In my own life, I think I can honestly say that out of the deepest pain has come the strongest conviction of the presence of God and the love of God."

MORE FROM GOD'S WORD ABOUT
SPIRITUAL GROWTH

But grow in the grace and knowledge of our Lord and Savior Jesus Christ. To Him be the glory both now and to the day of eternity.

2 Peter 3:18 HCSB

I want their hearts to be encouraged and joined together in love, so that they may have all the riches of assured understanding, and have the knowledge of God's mystery—Christ.

Colossians 2:2 HCSB

For You, O God, have tested us; You have refined us as silver is refined. You brought us into the net; You laid affliction on our backs. You have caused men to ride over our heads; we went through fire and through water; but You brought us out to rich fulfillment.

Psalm 66:10–12 NKJV

Now may the God of hope fill you with all joy and peace in believing, so that you may overflow with hope by the power of the Holy Spirit.

Romans 15:13 HCSB

MORE POWERFUL IDEAS ABOUT SPIRITUAL GROWTH

Your greatest ministry will likely come out of your greatest hurt.

Rick Warren

The vigor of our spiritual lives will be in exact proportion to the place held by the Bible in our lives and in our thoughts.

George Mueller

God's plan for our guidance is for us to grow gradually in wisdom before we get to the crossroads.

Bill Hybels

A Christian is never in a state of completion but always in the process of becoming.

Martin Luther

Virtually everything we see in the area of finances is little more than an external reflection of the internal spiritual condition.

Larry Burkett

QUESTIONS TO CONSIDER

Do I believe that God has lessons to teach me about money?

_____

_____

Do I believe that I still have "room to grow" in my faith?

_____

_____

Do I believe that spiritual growth usually happens day by day, and do I try to keep growing every day?

_____

_____

A PRAYER FOR TODAY

*Dear Lord, when I open myself to You,
I am blessed. Let me accept Your love and Your
wisdom, Father. Show me Your way, and deliver me
from the painful mistakes that I make when I stray
from Your commandments. Let me live according to
Your Word, and let me grow in my faith
every day that I live. Amen*

Day 7

TUNE IN TO GOD'S WORD

All Scripture is inspired by God and is profitable for teaching,
for rebuking, for correcting, for training in righteousness,
so that the man of God may be complete,
equipped for every good work.

2 Timothy 3:16-17 HCSB

THE FOCUS FOR TODAY

The strength that we claim from God's Word does not
depend on circumstances. Circumstances will be difficult,
but our strength will be sufficient.

Corrie ten Boom

The words of Matthew 4:4 remind us that, "Man shall not live by bread alone but by every word that proceedeth out of the mouth of God" (KJV). As believers, we must study the Bible and meditate upon its meaning for our lives. Otherwise, we deprive ourselves of a priceless gift from our Creator.

God's Word is unlike any other book. The Bible is a roadmap for life here on earth and for life eternal. As Christians, we are called upon to study God's Holy Word, to follow its commandments, and to share its Good News with the world.

Jonathan Edwards advised, "Be assiduous in reading the Holy Scriptures. This is the fountain whence all knowledge in divinity must be derived. Therefore let not this treasure lie by you neglected." God's Holy Word is, indeed, a priceless, one-of-a-kind treasure, and a passing acquaintance with the Good Book is insufficient for Christians who seek to obey God's Word and to understand His will. After all, man does not live by bread alone . . .

GOD'S WORD CONTAINS THE ANSWERS YOU NEED

If you're struggling with money problems, you're not alone. In today's easy-credit, buy-now-and-pay-later world, plenty of smart people have been caught in a money pit of debt and worry. So how can you escape that money pit as quickly and efficiently as possible? The answer, not surprisingly, can be found in the timeless wisdom of God's Holy Word. The quest for financial security is—and if you're a Christian, this should come as no surprise—largely a matter of applying a few Biblical principles early and often.

TODAY'S TIP FOR HANDLING TOUGH TIMES

If you have a decision to make, the Bible can help you make it. If you've got questions, the Bible has answers. If you're facing challenges, the Bible can help you overcome them. So take a Bible with you wherever you go. You never know when you may need a midday spiritual pick-me-up.

MORE FROM GOD'S WORD ABOUT GOD'S WORD

This is my comfort in my affliction, for Your word has given me life.

Psalm 119:50 NKJV

Let the Word of Christ—the Message—have the run of the house. Give it plenty of room in your lives. Instruct and direct one another using good common sense. And sing, sing your hearts out to God! Let every detail in your lives—words, actions, whatever—be done in the name of the Master, Jesus, thanking God the Father every step of the way.

Colossians 3:16-17 MSG

For the word of God is living and active. Sharper than any double-edged sword, it penetrates even to dividing soul and spirit, joints and marrow; it judges the thoughts and attitudes of the heart.

Hebrews 4:12 NIV

For as the rain comes down, and the snow from heaven, and do not return there, but water the earth, and make it bring forth and bud, that it may give seed to the sower and bread to the eater, so shall My word be that goes forth from My mouth; it shall not return to Me void, but it shall accomplish what I please, and it shall prosper in the thing for which I sent it.

Isaiah 55:10-11 NKJV

MORE POWERFUL IDEAS ABOUT GOD'S WORD

God has given us all sorts of counsel and direction in his written Word; thank God, we have it written down in black and white.

John Eldredge

Weave the fabric of God's word through your heart and mind. It will hold strong, even if the rest of life unravels.

Gigi Graham Tchividjian

The Bible is God's Word, given to us by God Himself so we can know Him and His will for our lives.

Billy Graham

Nobody ever outgrows Scripture; the book widens and deepens with our years.

C. H. Spurgeon

Prayer and the Word are inseparably linked together. Power in the use of either depends on the presence of the other.

Andrew Murray

If you want to know whether you're thinking correctly, check it out in the Word.

Charles Stanley

QUESTIONS TO CONSIDER

Do I make it a priority to read the Bible every day?

_____

_____

Do I consider regular Bible study to be an important source of wisdom?

_____

_____

Do I have a systematic plan for studying God's Word?

_____

_____

A PRAYER FOR TODAY

*Heavenly Father, Your Word is a light unto the world;
I will study it and trust it, and share it. In all that
I do, help me be a worthy witness for You as I share
the Good News of Your perfect Son
and Your perfect Word. Amen*

Day 8

YOUR NEW BUDGET

A sensible person sees danger and takes cover,
but the inexperienced keep going and are punished.

Proverbs 22:3 HCSB

THE FOCUS FOR TODAY

Budgeting is telling your money where to go
instead of asking it where it went.

John Maxwell

D o you have a written budget that tells you precisely where your money goes? If so, you've already taken an important step toward financial security. But if you don't have a budget, or if your budget is woefully out of date, please put down this book right now and begin writing the first draft of your new, improved, monthly household budget.

Far too many people "never quite get around" to making a budget. Why? Oftentimes, it's because these folks are afraid of the things that their budgets might reveal. Members of the non-budget crowd tell themselves that they're simply "too busy to budget" or that they're "bad with numbers." But in truth, these people are worried that their budgets might contain bad news; they're fearful that the cold hard facts may be too cold and too hard to take. But when it comes to money matters, ignorance is never bliss.

If you've been putting off the job of formulating your household budget, ask yourself why. And then, after that long embarrassing pause while you struggle, unsuccessfully, for a logical answer, start the budgeting process . . . now!

Creating a budget is relatively easy. Living by that budget can be considerably harder because life-on-a-budget demands discipline and self-sacrifice. If you find yourself struggling to live within your means, perhaps you need a significantly larger dose of wisdom from the ultimate guidebook on disciplined living: the Holy Bible.

Will regular readings of your Bible make you a financial genius? Probably not. The Bible is God's Holy Word; it is intended, first and foremost, as a tool for communicating God's plan of salvation to mankind. Nevertheless, the Bible can teach you how to become a more disciplined person. And, as you become disciplined in other aspects of your life, you will also become more disciplined in the management of your personal finances.

God's Word is clear: as a believer, you are called to lead a life of moderation, maturity, and discipline. But the world often tempts you to behave otherwise. Everywhere you turn, you will encounter powerful temptations to behave in undisciplined, intemperate, ungodly ways. And because you live in a world that glorifies material possessions, you will be tempted to squander your hard-earned money on a wide range of unnecessary purchases. Don't do it. Instead of spending now and worrying about it later, make a budget that makes sense. And live by it. When you do, you'll spend less time worrying and more time celebrating. And that, by the way, is precisely what God wants you to do.

BE REALISTIC

All too often, our written budgets contain too much hope and too little reality: It's easy to deceive ourselves with budgets that don't reflect the reality of our particular situations. If you have a budget that reflects positive cash flow but a bank account that contains little or no cash, it's time for a reality check.

TODAY'S TIP FOR HANDLING TOUGH TIMES

Budgeting Basics 101: Your budget should be realistic; it should be written down on paper; it should be created in cooperation with your spouse (if you have one); and it should be reviewed and updated regularly.

MORE FROM GOD'S WORD ABOUT DISCIPLINE

No discipline seems enjoyable at the time, but painful. Later on, however, it yields the fruit of peace and righteousness to those who have been trained by it.

Hebrews 12:11 HCSB

I discipline my body and bring it under strict control, so that after preaching to others, I myself will not be disqualified.

1 Corinthians 9:27 HCSB

The one who follows instruction is on the path to life, but the one who rejects correction goes astray.

Proverbs 10:17 HCSB

For this very reason, make every effort to supplement your faith with goodness, goodness with knowledge, knowledge with self-control, self-control with endurance, endurance with godliness.

2 Peter 1:5-6 HCSB

Therefore by their fruits you will know them.

Matthew 7:20 NKJV

57

MORE POWERFUL IDEAS ABOUT
PLANNING, DISCIPLINE, AND THRIFT

By failing to prepare, you are preparing to fail.

Ben Franklin

God cannot build character without our cooperation. If we resist Him, then He chastens us into submission. But, if we submit to Him, then He can accomplish His work. He is not satisfied with a halfway job. God wants a perfect work; He wants a finished product that is mature and complete.

Warren Wiersbe

As we seek to become disciples of Jesus Christ, we should never forget that the word disciple is directly related to the word discipline. To be a disciple of the Lord Jesus Christ is to know his discipline.

Dennis Swanberg

You cannot bring about prosperity by discouraging thrift.

William Boetcker

Christians have become victims of one of the most devious plots Satan ever created—the concept that money belongs to us and not to God.

Larry Burkett

Work is doing it.
Discipline is doing it every day.
Diligence is doing it
well every day.

—

Dave Ramsey

QUESTIONS TO CONSIDER

In the space below, make a list of at least five ways that
you and your family will be helped when you establish a
sensible budget and stick to it.

1. _____

_____

2. _____

_____

3. _____

_____

4. _____

_____

5. _____

_____

A PRAYER FOR TODAY

*Dear Lord, give me the wisdom to plan my life
carefully, to share my possessions joyfully,
and accept my blessings thankfully. Amen*

Day 9

LIVE AT A PROFIT

For you need endurance, so that after you have done
God's will, you may receive what was promised.

Hebrews 10:36 HCSB

THE FOCUS FOR TODAY

If a person gets his attitude toward money straight,
it will help straighten out almost
every other area of his life.

Billy Graham

S pending money is an incredibly easy thing to do. After all, the shopping malls and discount stores are filled to the ceilings with attractively packaged items, all of which were created for a single purpose: so that we, the consuming public, might buy them.

But when we spend more than we should—when we become overly absorbed with the acquisition of things—complications arise. Each new acquisition costs money or time, often both. To further complicate matters, many items can be purchased, not with real money, but with something much more insidious: debt. Debt—especially consumer debt used to purchase items that immediately go down in value—is a modern-day form of indentured servitude.

If you're looking for a sure-fire, time-tested way to simplify your life and thereby improve your world, learn to control your possessions before they control you. Purchase only those things that make a significant contribution to your well being and the well being of your family. Never spend more than you make. Understand the folly in buying consumer goods on credit. Never use credit cards as a way of financing your lifestyle.

Ask yourself this simple question: "Do I own my possessions, or do they own me?" If you don't like the answer you receive, make an ironclad promise to stop acquiring and start divesting. Make up your mind to live at a profit, even if that means making radical changes in the way you spend money.

When you begin spending less, you'll be amazed at the things you can do without. You'll be pleasantly surprised at the sense of satisfaction that accompanies your newfound moderation. And you'll understand first-hand that when it comes to material possessions, less truly is more.

SELF-DISCIPLINE IS REQUIRED

You've probably heard this advice on thousands of occasions: "Spend less than you make." It sounds so easy, but it can be so hard. After all, we live in a world that is filled to the brim with wonderful things to buy and wonderful people telling us that we need to buy those things. But sometimes, our desires for more and better stuff can overload our ability to pay for the things we want. That's when Old Man Trouble arrives at the door.

The answer to the problem of overspending is straight-forward. What's required is discipline. First, we must earn money through honest work for which we are well suited; then, we must spend less than we earn (and save the rest intelligently). This strategy of earning and saving money is simple to understand but much harder to put into practice. Thankfully, God gave us clear instructions that, when followed, can lead us on the proper path.

God's Word reminds us again and again that our Creator expects us to lead disciplined lives. God doesn't reward laziness, misbehavior, or apathy. To the contrary, He expects us to behave with dignity and discipline. But ours is a world in which dignity and discipline are often in short supply.

We live in a world in which leisure is glorified and indifference is often glamorized. But God has other plans. God gives us talents and He expects us to use them. Of course, it is seldom easy to cultivate those talents. Sometimes, we must invest countless hours (or, in some cases, many years) honing our skills. And that's perfectly okay with God, because He understands that self-discipline is a blessing, not a burden.

When we pause to consider how much work needs to be done, we realize that self-discipline is not simply a proven way to get ahead, it's also an integral part of God's plan for our lives. If we genuinely seek to be faithful stewards of our time, our talents, and our resources, we must adopt a disciplined approach to life. There's simply no other way.

TODAY'S TIP FOR HANDLING TOUGH TIMES

If you spend more than you make, you're sending Old Man Trouble an engraved invitation to become an integral part of your life—and that's a very big mistake. So do yourself a favor: make whatever sacrifices are required to live at a profit.

MORE FROM GOD'S WORD ABOUT SPENDING LESS

For the love of money is a root of all kinds of evil, for which some have strayed from the faith in their greediness, and pierced themselves through with many sorrows. But you, O man of God, flee these things and pursue righteousness, godliness, faith, love, patience, gentleness.

1 Timothy 6:10–11 NKJV

Don't collect for yourselves treasures on earth, where moth and rust destroy and where thieves break in and steal. But collect for yourselves treasures in heaven, where neither moth nor rust destroys, and where thieves don't break in and steal. For where your treasure is, there your heart will be also.

Matthew 6:19-21 HCSB

And He said to them,
"Take heed and beware of covetousness,
for one's life does not consist in
the abundance of the things he possesses."

—

Luke 12:15 NKJV

More Powerful Ideas About Overspending

There is nothing wrong with people possessing riches. The wrong comes when riches possess people.

Billy Graham

Money is a mirror that, strange as it sounds, reflects our personal weaknesses and strengths with amazing clarity.

Dave Ramsey

Have you prayed about your resources lately? Find out how God wants you to use your time and your money. No matter what it costs, forsake all that is not of God.

Kay Arthur

No test of a man's true character is more conclusive than how he spends his time and his money.

Patrick Morley

Men do not realize how great a revenue economy is.

Cicero

Beware of little expenses. A small leak will sink a big ship.

Ben Franklin

QUESTIONS TO CONSIDER

In the space below, take a moment to describe your spending habits: how you've spent money in the past, how you're spending it now, and how you plan to spend it in the future.

_____

_____

_____

_____

_____

_____

_____

_____

_____

_____

A PRAYER FOR TODAY

*Dear Lord, help me think sensibly about money.
And let me always remember that my greatest
possession has nothing to do with my checkbook;
my greatest possession is my relationship with You
through Jesus Christ. Amen*

Day 10

GUARDING YOUR THOUGHTS

*Finally brothers, whatever is true, whatever is honorable,
whatever is just, whatever is pure, whatever is lovely,
whatever is commendable—if there is any moral excellence
and if there is any praise—dwell on these things.*

Philippians 4:8 HCSB

THE FOCUS FOR TODAY

Your thoughts are the determining factor as to whose
mold you are conformed to. Control your thoughts
and you control the direction of your life.

Charles Stanley

Even when you're facing tough challenges, are you an optimistic, hopeful, enthusiastic Christian? You should be. After all, as a believer, you have every reason to be optimistic about life here on earth and life eternal. As English clergyman William Ralph Inge observed, "No Christian should be a pessimist, for Christianity is a system of radical optimism." Inge's words are most certainly true, but sometimes, you may find yourself pulled down by tough times. If you find yourself discouraged, exhausted, or both, then it's time to ask yourself this question: what's bothering you, and why?

If you're worried by the inevitable challenges of everyday living, God wants to have a little talk with you. After all, the ultimate battle has already been won on the cross at Calvary. And if your life has been transformed by Christ's sacrifice, then you, as a recipient of God's grace, have every reason to live courageously.

Are you willing to trust God's plans for your life, in good times and hard times? Hopefully, you will trust Him completely. Proverbs 3:5-6 makes it clear: "Trust in the Lord with all your heart, and lean not on your own understanding; in all your ways acknowledge Him, and He shall direct your paths" (NKJV).

A. W. Tozer noted, "Attitude is all-important. Let the soul take a quiet attitude of faith and love toward God, and from there on, the responsibility is God's. He will make good on His commitments." These words should serve as a reminder that even when the challenges of the day seem daunting, God remains steadfast. And, so should you.

So make this promise to yourself and keep it—vow to be a hope-filled Christian. Think optimistically about your life, your profession, your family, your future, and your purpose for living. Trust your hopes, not your fears. Take time to celebrate God's glorious creation. And then, when you've filled your heart with hope and gladness, share your optimism with others. They'll be better for it, and so will you.

TODAY'S TIP FOR HANDLING TOUGH TIMES

Be a realistic optimist. Your attitude toward the future will help create your future. So think realistically about yourself and your situation while making a conscious effort to focus on hopes, not fears. When you do, you'll put the self-fulfilling prophecy to work for you.

MORE FROM GOD'S WORD ABOUT YOUR THOUGHTS

Come near to God, and God will come near to you. You sinners, clean sin out of your lives. You who are trying to follow God and the world at the same time, make your thinking pure.

James 4:8 NCV

Those who are pure in their thinking are happy, because they will be with God.

Matthew 5:8 NCV

Do not conform any longer to the pattern of this world, but be transformed by the renewing of your mind. Then you will be able to test and approve what God's will is—his good, pleasing and perfect will.

Romans 12:2 NIV

So prepare your minds for service and have self-control.

1 Peter 1:13 NCV

Dear friend, guard Clear Thinking and Common Sense with your life; don't for a minute lose sight of them. They'll keep your soul alive and well, they'll keep you fit and attractive.

Proverbs 3:21-22 MSG

MORE POWERFUL IDEAS ABOUT
THE POWER OF YOUR THOUGHTS

The things we think are the things that feed our souls. If we think on pure and lovely things, we shall grow pure and lovely like them; and the converse is equally true.

Hannah Whitall Smith

Every major spiritual battle is in the mind.

Charles Stanley

It is the thoughts and intents of the heart that shape a person's life.

John Eldredge

People who do not develop and practice good thinking often find themselves at the mercy of their circumstances.

John Maxwell

I became aware of one very important concept I had missed before: my attitude—not my circumstances—was what was making me unhappy.

Vonette Bright

Attitude is the mind's paintbrush; it can color any situation.

Barbara Johnson

QUESTIONS TO CONSIDER

Do I understand the importance of directing my thoughts in a proper direction?

_____

_____

Do I believe that emotions are contagious, and do I try to associate with people who are upbeat, optimistic, and encouraging?

_____

_____

Do I understand that when I dwell on positive thoughts, I feel better about myself and my circumstances?

_____

_____

A PRAYER FOR TODAY

Dear Lord, I will focus on Your love, Your power, Your Promises, and Your Son. When I am weak, I will turn to You for strength; when I am worried, I will turn to You for comfort; when I am troubled, I will turn to You for patience and perspective. Help me guard my thoughts, Lord, so that I may honor You this day and forever. Amen

Day 11

SIMPLICITY IS GENIUS: DISCOVERING THE THINGS YOU CAN LIVE WITHOUT

But godliness with contentment is a great gain. For we brought nothing into the world, and we can take nothing out. But if we have food and clothing, we will be content with these. But those who want to be rich fall into temptation, a trap, and many foolish and harmful desires, which plunge people into ruin and destruction.

1 Timothy 6:6-9 HCSB

THE FOCUS FOR TODAY

Prescription for a happier and healthier life: resolve to slow down your pace; learn to say no gracefully; resist the temptation to chase after more pleasure, more hobbies, and more social entanglements.

James Dobson

You live in a world where simplicity is in short supply. Think for a moment about the complexity of your life and compare it to the lives of your ancestors. Certainly, you are the beneficiary of many technological innovations, but these innovations have a price: in all likelihood, your world is highly complex. Consider the following:

1. From the moment you wake up in the morning until the time you lay your head on the pillow at night, you are the target of an endless stream of advertising information. Each message is intended to grab your attention in order to convince you to purchase things you didn't know you needed (and probably don't!). 2. Essential aspects of your life, including personal matters such as health care, are subject to an ever-increasing flood of rules and regulations. 3. Unless you take firm control of your time and your life, you may be overwhelmed by a tidal wave of complexity that threatens your happiness.

Is yours a life of moderation or accumulation? Are you more interested in the possessions you can acquire or in the person you can become? The answers to these questions will determine the direction of your day and, in time, the direction of your life.

If your material possessions are somehow distancing you from God, discard them. If your outside interests leave you too little time for your family or your Creator, slow down the merry-go-round, or better yet, get off the merry-go-round completely. Remember: God wants your full attention, and He wants it today, so don't let anybody or anything get in His way.

SIMPLICITY IS BEAUTIFUL

If your mailbox is overflowing with credit card bills and your bank balance is approaching single digits, it's officially time to simplify your life. But before you unload that seldom-used food processor at your next yard sale, toss your credit cards into the blender and push "Liquefy."

TODAY'S TIP FOR HANDLING TOUGH TIMES

Perhaps you think that the more stuff you acquire, the happier you'll be. If so, think again. Too much stuff means too many headaches, so start simplifying now.

MORE FROM GOD'S WORD ABOUT SIMPLICITY

A pretentious, showy life is an empty life; a plain and simple life is a full life.

Proverbs 13:7 MSG

You've gotten a reputation as a bad-news people, you people of Judah and Israel, but I'm coming to save you. From now on, you're the good-news people. Don't be afraid. Keep a firm grip on what I'm doing.

Zechariah 8:13 MSG

A simple life in the Fear-of-God is better than a rich life with a ton of headaches.

Proverbs 15:16 MSG

But he's already made it plain how to live, what to do, what God is looking for in men and women. It's quite simple: Do what is fair and just to your neighbor, be compassionate and loyal in your love, and don't take yourself too seriously—take God seriously.

Micah 6:8 MSG

And let the peace of God rule in your hearts . . . and be ye thankful.

Colossians 3:15 KJV

MORE POWERFUL IDEAS ABOUT SIMPLICITY

Distractions must be conquered or they will conquer us. So let us cultivate simplicity; let us want fewer things; let us walk in the Spirit; let us fill our minds with the Word of God and our hearts with praise.

A. W. Tozer

There is no correlation between wealth and happiness.

Larry Burkett

The most powerful life is the most simple life. The most powerful life is the life that knows where it's going, that knows where the source of strength is; it is the life that stays free of clutter and happenstance and hurriedness.

Max Lucado

The characteristic of the life of a saint is essentially elemental simplicity.

Oswald Chambers

He is rich that is satisfied.

Thomas Fuller

If you desire many things, many things will seem but a few.

Ben Franklin

QUESTIONS TO CONSIDER

In the space below, make a list of at least of at least three things that you can do today to start simplifying your life.

1. _____

_____

_____

_____

2. _____

_____

_____

_____

3. _____

_____

_____

_____

A PRAYER FOR TODAY

Dear Lord, help me understand the joys of simplicity.
Life is complicated enough without my adding to
the confusion. Wherever I happen to be,
help me to keep it simple—very simple. Amen

Day 12

TIME TO GET BUSY

And whatever you do, do it heartily,
as to the Lord and not to men.
Colossians 3:23 NKJV

THE FOCUS FOR TODAY

Let us not be content to wait and see what will happen,
but give us the determination to make
the right things happen.

Peter Marshall

I t isn't easy to overcome tough times—it takes hard work and lots of it. So if you're facing financial challenges of any kind, you can be sure that God has important work for you to do . . . but He won't make you do it. Since the days of Adam and Eve, God has allowed His children to make choices for themselves, and so it is with you. You can either dig in and work hard, or you can retreat to the couch, click on the TV, and hope things get better on their own.

The Bible instructs us that we can learn an important lesson of a surprising source: ants. Ants are among nature's most industrious creatures. They do their work without supervision, rumination, or hesitation. We should do likewise. When times are tough, we must summon the courage and determination to work ourselves out of trouble.

God has created a world in which diligence is rewarded and sloth is not. So whatever you choose to do, do it with commitment, excitement, and vigor. God didn't create you for a life of mediocrity or pain; He created you for far greater things. Reaching for greater things—and defeating tough times—usually requires work and lots of it, which is perfectly fine with God. After all, He knows that you're up to the task, and He still has big plans for you. Very big plans . . .

WHEREVER YOU ARE, WORK HARD

Wherever you find yourself, whatever your job description, do your work, and do it with all your heart. When you do, you will most certainly win the recognition of your peers. But more importantly, God will bless your efforts and use you in ways that only He can understand. So do your work with focus and dedication. And leave the rest up to God.

TODAY'S TIP FOR HANDLING TOUGH TIMES

Today, pick out one important obligation that you've been putting off. Then, take at least one specific step toward the completion of the task you've been avoiding. Even if you don't finish the work completely, you'll discover that it's easier to finish a task that you've already begun than to finish a job you've never started.

MORE FROM GOD'S WORD ABOUT
THE NEED TO TAKE ACTION

For the Kingdom of God is not just fancy talk; it is living by God's power.

1 Corinthians 4:20 NLT

Therefore, get your minds ready for action, being self-disciplined, and set your hope completely on the grace to be brought to you at the revelation of Jesus Christ.

1 Peter 1:13 HCSB

But prove yourselves doers of the word, and not merely hearers.

James 1:22 NASB

Are there those among you who are truly wise and understanding? Then they should show it by living right and doing good things with a gentleness that comes from wisdom.

James 3:13 NCV

The prudent see danger and take refuge, but the simple keep going and suffer from it.

Proverbs 27:12 NIV

MORE POWERFUL IDEAS ABOUT
THE NEED TO TAKE ACTION

Action springs not from thought, but from a readiness for responsibility.

Dietrich Bonhoeffer

God has lots of folks who intend to go to work for Him "some day." What He needs is more people who are willing to work for Him this day.

Marie T. Freeman

Paul did one thing. Most of us dabble in forty things. Are you a doer or a dabbler?

Vance Havner

Logic will not change an emotion, but action will.

Zig Ziglar

It is by acts and not by ideas that people live.

Harry Emerson Fosdick

Pray as if it's all up to God, and work as if it's all up to you.

Anonymous

QUESTIONS TO CONSIDER

When I have work that needs to be done, do I usually try to finish the work as soon as possible, or do I put it off?

_____

_____

Do I believe that my testimony is more powerful when actions accompany my words?

_____

_____

Do I see the hypocrisy in saying one thing and doing another, and do I try my best to act in accordance with my beliefs?

_____

_____

A PRAYER FOR TODAY

Heavenly Father, when I am fearful, keep me mindful that You are my protector and my salvation. Give me strength, Lord, to face the challenges of this day as I gain my courage from You. Amen

DON'T BECOME A PRISONER TO ANGER OR REGRET

And don't be wishing you were someplace else or with someone else. Where you are right now is God's place for you. Live and obey and love and believe right there.

1 Corinthians 7:17 MSG

THE FOCUS FOR TODAY

Get rid of the poison of built-up anger and the acid of long-term resentment.

Charles Swindoll

A re you caught in the quicksand of regret? Have tough financial times left you bound up by the bonds of bitterness? Do you find it impossible to forgive others for the wrongs they may have done to you? If so, be forewarned: you are not only disobeying your Heavenly Father, but you are also wasting your time. The world holds few if any rewards for those who remain angrily focused upon past injustices. And neither, for that matter, does God.

God's Word is clear. In the 43rd chapter of Isaiah, we read: "The Lord says, 'Forget what happened before, and do not think about the past. Look at the new thing I am going to do. It is already happening. Don't you see it? I will make a road in the desert and rivers in the dry land'" (v. 18-19 NCV). Yet most of us have great difficulty forgetting "what happened before." Instead of entrusting the past to God, we dwell upon our misfortunes. The irony of our shortsightedness is this: by allowing ourselves to become embittered by our disappointments, we inevitably set ourselves up for even more disappointments in the future. Why? Because bitter hearts yield bitter fruits (Luke 6:44-45).

Bitterness is a spiritual sickness that can consume us if we let it. Our challenge, as responsible believers who seek to walk with God, is this: we must train ourselves to think—and to pray—in ways that remove the poison of bitterness from our hearts.

If you are caught up in intense feelings of anger or resentment, you know all too well the destructive power of these emotions. How can you rid yourself of these feelings? First, you must prayerfully ask God to cleanse your heart. Then, you must learn to catch yourself whenever feelings of anger or bitterness to invade your thoughts. In short, you must learn to recognize and to resist negative thoughts before they hijack your emotions.

If there exists even one person—alive or dead—against whom you hold bitter feelings, it's time to forgive. Or, if you are embittered against yourself for some past mistake or shortcoming, it's finally time to forgive yourself and move on. Remember that bitterness is not part of God's plan for your life, so pray, think, and forgive accordingly.

TODAY'S TIP FOR HANDLING TOUGH TIMES

If financial hardships have left you focused on the past, it's time to refocus your thoughts on the responsibilities of today and the opportunities of tomorrow.

MORE FROM GOD'S WORD ABOUT REGRET

Do not remember the past events, pay no attention to things of old. Look, I am about to do something new; even now it is coming. Do you not see it? Indeed, I will make a way in the wilderness, rivers in the desert.

Isaiah 43:18-19 HCSB

One thing I do, forgetting those things which are behind and reaching forward to those things which are ahead, I press toward the goal for the prize of the upward call of God in Christ Jesus.

Philippians 3:13-14 NKJV

Consider it a great joy, my brothers, whenever you experience various trials, knowing that the testing of your faith produces endurance. But endurance must do its complete work, so that you may be mature and complete, lacking nothing.

James 1:2-4 HCSB

Now everything is from God, who reconciled us to Himself through Christ and gave us the ministry of reconciliation.

2 Corinthians 5:18 HCSB

MORE POWERFUL IDEAS ABOUT REGRET

Our yesterdays present irreparable things to us; it is true that we have lost opportunities which will never return, but God can transform this destructive anxiety into a constructive thoughtfulness for the future. Let the past sleep, but let it sleep on the bosom of Christ. Leave the Irreparable Past in His hands, and step out into the Irresistible Future with Him.

Oswald Chambers

In the Christian story God descends to reascend. He comes down; . . . down to the very roots and sea-bed of the Nature He has created. But He goes down to come up again and bring the whole ruined world with Him.

C. S. Lewis

The enemy of our souls loves to taunt us with past failures, wrongs, disappointments, disasters, and calamities. And if we let him continue doing this, our life becomes a long and dark tunnel, with very little light at the end.

Charles Swindoll

We need to be at peace with our past, content with our present, and sure about our future, knowing they are all in God's hands.

Joyce Meyer

QUESTIONS TO CONSIDER

Am I able to learn from the past and to accept the past, but to live in the present?

_____

_____

Do I believe that it is important to trust God even when I don't understand why certain things happen?

_____

_____

Am I willing to change the things I can change and accept the things I can't?

_____

_____

A PRAYER FOR TODAY

Heavenly Father, free me from anger, resentment, and envy. When I am bitter, I cannot feel the peace that You intend for my life. Keep me mindful that forgiveness is Your commandment, and help me accept the past, treasure the present, and trust the future . . . to You. Amen

Day 14

TO STAY SANE, KEEP MONEY IN PERSPECTIVE

*For the love of money is a root of all kinds of evil, for which
some have strayed from the faith in their greediness,
and pierced themselves through with many sorrows. But you,
O man of God, flee these things and pursue righteousness,
godliness, faith, love, patience, gentleness.*

1 Timothy 6:10-11 NKJV

THE FOCUS FOR TODAY

No man can stand in front of Jesus Christ
and say "I want to make money."

Oswald Chambers

The Bible clearly warns us that the love of money is "a root of all kinds of evil." So when we consider ways to save money and accumulate wealth, we must beware. Money, in and of itself, is not evil, but worshipping money is.

Are you placing too high a priority on money? Are you more focused on your next paycheck than you are on God? Do you spend more time thinking about your next acquisition than you do about God's plan for your life? If so, it's time to talk seriously to God about your priorities.

Today, as you prioritize matters of importance for you and yours, remember that God is almighty, but the dollar is not. If we worship God, we are blessed. But if we worship "the almighty dollar," we are inevitably punished because of our misplaced priorities—and our punishment inevitably comes sooner rather than later.

ASK GOD TO GIVE YOU PERSPECTIVE

If a temporary loss of perspective has left you worried, exhausted, or both, it's time to readjust your thought patterns. Negative thoughts are habit-forming; thankfully, so are positive ones. With practice, you can form the habit of focusing on God's priorities and your own possibilities.

When you do, you'll soon discover that you will spend less time fretting about your challenges and more time praising God for His gifts.

When you call upon the Lord and prayerfully seek His will, He will give you wisdom and perspective. When you make God's priorities your priorities, He will direct your steps and calm your fears. So today and every day hereafter, pray for a sense of balance and perspective. And remember: no problems are too big for God—and that includes yours.

TODAY'S TIP FOR HANDLING TOUGH TIMES

When you realize that this world is not your home, that realization changes the way you think about money . . . and the way you spend it.

MORE FROM GOD'S WORD ABOUT PERSPECTIVE

Now if any of you lacks wisdom, he should ask God, who gives to all generously and without criticizing, and it will be given to him.

James 1:5 HCSB

For now we see in a mirror, dimly, but then face to face. Now I know in part, but then I shall know just as I also am known.

1 Corinthians 13:12 NKJV

Let no one deceive himself. If anyone among you seems to be wise in this age, let him become a fool that he may become wise. For the wisdom of this world is foolishness with God. For it is written, "He catches the wise in their own craftiness."

1 Corinthians 3:18-19 NKJV

Acquire wisdom—how much better it is than gold! And acquire understanding—it is preferable to silver.

Proverbs 16:16 HCSB

The one who acquires good sense loves himself; one who safeguards understanding finds success.

Proverbs 19:8 HCSB

MORE POWERFUL IDEAS ABOUT KEEPING THINGS IN PERSPECTIVE

Earthly fears are no fears at all. Answer the big questions of eternity, and the little questions of life fall into perspective.

Max Lucado

Instead of being frustrated and overwhelmed by all that is going on in our world, go to the Lord and ask Him to give you His eternal perspective.

Kay Arthur

The proper perspective creates within us a spirit of reaching outside of ourselves with joy and enthusiasm.

Luci Swindoll

What you see and hear depends a good deal on where you are standing; it also depends on what sort of person you are.

C. S. Lewis

If we believe that God really loves us and will give us only the amount of money that we can handle without worry, we can have perfect peace in finances.

Larry Burkett

QUESTIONS TO CONSIDER

Do I understand the importance of keeping financial concerns in proper perspective?

_____

_____

Do I realize that even when I have financial challenges, I am still richly blessed?

_____

_____

Do I understand that God still has important lessons to teach me?

_____

_____

A PRAYER FOR TODAY

*Dear Lord, I will earn money and I will use money,
but I will not worship money. Give me the wisdom and
the discipline to be a responsible steward of my financial
resources, and let me use those resources for the glory
of Your kingdom. Amen*

DON'T GIVE UP ON YOURSELF OR ON GOD

No matter how many times you trip them up,
God-loyal people don't stay down long;
Soon they're up on their feet,
while the wicked end up flat on their faces.

Proverbs 24:16 MSG

THE FOCUS FOR TODAY

As we wait on God, He helps us use the winds of
adversity to soar above our problems.
As the Bible says, "Those who wait on the LORD . . .
shall mount up with wings like eagles."

Billy Graham

The old saying is as true today as it was when it was first spoken: "Life is a marathon, not a sprint." That's why wise travelers (like you) select a traveling companion who never tires and never falters. That partner, of course, is your Heavenly Father.

The next time you find your courage tested to the limit, remember that God is as near as your next breath, and remember that He offers strength and comfort to His children. He is your shield and your strength; He is your protector and your deliverer. Call upon Him in your hour of need and then be comforted. Whatever your challenge, whatever your trouble, God can help you persevere. And that's precisely what He'll do if you ask Him.

Perhaps you are in a hurry for God to help you resolve your financial challenges. Perhaps you're anxious to earn the rewards that you feel you've already earned from life. Perhaps you're drumming your fingers, impatiently waiting for God to act. If so, be forewarned: God operates on His own timetable, not yours. Sometimes, God may answer your prayers with silence, and when He does, you must patiently persevere. In times of trouble, you must remain steadfast and trust in the merciful goodness of your Heavenly Father. Whatever your problem, He can handle it. Your job is to keep persevering until He does.

Keep your eyes on Jesus, who both began and finished
this race we're in. Study how he did it.
Because he never lost sight of where he was headed—
that exhilarating finish in and with God—
he could put up with anything along the way:
cross, shame, whatever. And now he's there,
in the place of honor, right alongside God.

—

Hebrews 12:2 MSG

TODAY'S TIP FOR HANDLING TOUGH TIMES

Focus on possibilities, not roadblocks. The road of life contains a number of potholes and stumbling blocks. Of course you will encounter them from time to time, and so will your family members. But, don't invest large quantities of your life focusing on past misfortunes. On the road of life, regret is a dead end.

MORE FROM GOD'S WORD ABOUT PERSEVERANCE

Let us not become weary in doing good, for at the proper time we will reap a harvest if we do not give up.

Galatians 6:9 NIV

For you have need of endurance, so that when you have done the will of God, you may receive what was promised.

Hebrews 10:36 NASB

Thanks be to God! He gives us the victory through our Lord Jesus Christ. Therefore, my dear brothers, stand firm. Let nothing move you. Always give yourselves fully to the work of the Lord, because you know that your labor in the Lord is not in vain.

1 Corinthians 15:57-58 NIV

Be diligent that ye may be found of him in peace, without spot, and blameless.

2 Peter 3:14 KJV

It is better to finish something than to start it. It is better to be patient than to be proud.

Ecclesiastes 7:8 NCV

More Powerful Ideas About Perseverance

We don't give up. We look up. We trust. We believe. And our optimism is not hollow. Christ has proven worthy. He has shown that he never fails. That's what makes God, God.

Max Lucado

In all negotiations of difficulties, a man may not look to sow and reap at once. He must prepare his business and so ripen it by degrees.

Francis Bacon

Are you a Christian? If you are, how can you be hopeless? Are you so depressed by the greatness of your problems that you have given up all hope? Instead of giving up, would you patiently endure? Would you focus on Christ until you are so preoccupied with him alone that you fall prostrate before him?

Anne Graham Lotz

Failure is one of life's most powerful teachers. How we handle our failures determines whether we're going to simply "get by" in life or "press on."

Beth Moore

QUESTIONS TO CONSIDER

Do I have a healthy respect for the power of perseverance?

_____

_____

When I am discouraged, do I ask God to give me strength?

_____

_____

Do I associate with people who encourage me to be courageous, optimistic, energetic, and persistent?

_____

_____

A PRAYER FOR TODAY

Dear Lord, all I have belongs to You.
When I leave this world I take nothing with me.
Help me to value my relationship with You—
and my relationships with others—more than
I value my material possessions. Amen

Day 16

Don't Get Trapped in the Material World

*And He told them, "Watch out and be on guard
against all greed, because one's life is not in
the abundance of his possessions."*
Luke 12:15 HCSB

The Focus for Today

The more we stuff ourselves with material pleasures,
the less we seem to appreciate life.
Barbara Johnson

I n our modern society, we need money to live. But as Christians, we must never make the acquisition of money the central focus of our lives. Money is a tool, but it should never overwhelm our sensibilities. The focus of life must be squarely on things spiritual, not things material.

Whenever we place our love for material possessions above our love for God—or when we yield to the countless other temptations of everyday living—we find ourselves engaged in a struggle between good and evil. Let us respond to this struggle by freeing ourselves from that subtle yet powerful temptation: the temptation to love the world more than we love God.

Whenever we become absorbed with the acquisition of things, complications arise. Each new acquisition costs money or time, often both. To further complicate matters, many items can be purchased, not with real money, but with the something much more insidious: debt. Debt—especially consumer debt used to purchase depreciating assets—is a modern-day form of indentured servitude. So do yourself and your family a favor: Pay as you go. In other words, don't buy stuff—especially expensive consumer items that quickly go down in value—unless you have the money to pay for them in your bank account.

Want a boat? Save up until you can comfortably afford to pay for it in cash. Want to take a cruise to the Bahamas?

Ditto. Like to impress your neighbors with a brand new big-screen TV? Don't buy it on the "easy-pay" plan. Either pay for it in cash right now (if you can) . . . or keep watching your little TV. And while you're at it, think long and hard about the role that material possessions play in your life—and the role that they should play.

How important are our material possessions? Not as important as we might think. In the lives of committed Christians, material possessions should play a rather small role. Of course, we all need the basic necessities of life, but once we meet those needs for ourselves and for our families, the piling up of possessions creates more problems than it solves. Our real riches, of course, are not of this world. We are never really rich until we are rich in spirit.

So, if you find yourself wrapped up in the concerns of the material world, it's time to reorder your priorities by turning your thoughts and your prayers to more important matters. And, it's time to begin storing up riches that will endure throughout eternity: the spiritual kind.

TODAY'S TIP FOR HANDLING TOUGH TIMES

Material possessions may seem appealing at first, but they pale in comparison to the spiritual gifts that God gives to those who put Him first. Count yourself among that number.

MORE FROM GOD'S WORD ABOUT MATERIALISM

For what does it benefit a man to gain the whole world yet lose his life? What can a man give in exchange for his life?

Mark 8:36-37 HCSB

Don't collect for yourselves treasures on earth, where moth and rust destroy and where thieves break in and steal. But collect for yourselves treasures in heaven, where neither moth nor rust destroys, and where thieves don't break in and steal. For where your treasure is, there your heart will be also.

Matthew 6:19-21 HCSB

Anyone trusting in his riches will fall, but the righteous will flourish like foliage.

Proverbs 11:28 HCSB

For the mind-set of the flesh is death, but the mind-set of the Spirit is life and peace.

Romans 8:6 HCSB

Love not the world, neither the things that are in the world. If any man love the world, the love of the Father is not in him.

1 John 2:15 KJV

MORE POWERFUL IDEAS ABOUT MATERIALISM

If you want to be truly happy, you won't find it on an endless quest for more stuff. You'll find it in receiving God's generosity and in the passing that generosity along.

Bill Hybels

It's sobering to contemplate how much time, effort, sacrifice, compromise, and attention we give to acquiring and increasing our supply of something that is totally insignificant in eternity.

Anne Graham Lotz

There is absolutely no evidence that complexity and materialism lead to happiness. On the contrary, there is plenty of evidence that simplicity and spirituality lead to joy, a blessedness that is better than happiness.

Dennis Swanberg

The cross is laid on every Christian. It begins with the call to abandon the attachments of this world.

Dietrich Bonhoeffer

As faithful stewards of what we have, ought we not to give earnest thought to our staggering surplus?

Elisabeth Elliot

QUESTIONS TO CONSIDER

Do I understand the importance of keeping material possessions in proper perspective?

_____

_____

In the past, have I overestimated the importance of money and underestimated the importance of other things?

_____

_____

When times are tough, do I focus on the things I don't have and forget to thank God for the things I do have?

_____

_____

A PRAYER FOR TODAY

*Heavenly Father, when I focus intently upon You,
I am blessed. When I focus too intently on the
acquisition of material possessions, I am troubled.
Make my priorities pleasing to You, Father,
and make me a worthy servant of Your Son. Amen*

UNDERSTANDING DEBT: SOCIETY'S VALUES VERSUS GOD'S VALUES

The borrower is servant to the lender.

Proverbs 22:7 NLT

THE FOCUS FOR TODAY

Too many people buy things on the "lay-awake" plan.

Dave Ramsey

We live in a world that has become so reliant upon debt that our entire economy depends upon it. How many new automobiles would dealers sell if there were no car loans? Not very many. And how many businesses would cease operations if their short term credit lines were "called" tomorrow? Plenty! Face it: we live in a world that is addicted to debt, but you needn't be. Just because our world revolves around borrowed money doesn't mean that you must do likewise.

Of course, not all debt is dangerous to your financial health. If you borrow money to purchase a well-located home—if you make a sensible down payment, and if you can comfortably afford all the expenses of owning and maintaining your residence—then you're probably making a wise decision by becoming a homeowner. Why? Because home mortgage debt, when used judiciously, can have a positive influence on your financial wellbeing. But other forms of debt are not so benign.

If you're already living beyond your means and borrowing to pay for the privilege, then you know that sleepless nights and stress-filled days are the psychological payments that must be extracted from those who buy too much "now" in hopes that they can pay for those things "later." Unfortunately, "later" usually arrives sooner than expected, and that's when the trouble begins.

Everywhere you turn, businesses are trying to convince you to become their debtor. Credit cards (which are advertised as "low-interest," but aren't) are easy to acquire, even easier to use, and, at times, incredibly difficult to pay off. In fact, excessive credit card debt has brought untold misery to countless families, and it's your job to ensure that your family is spared from this needless suffering.

Sometimes, you don't need a credit card to get yourself into trouble. Offers of "zero-down" or "zero-percent financing," which are designed to let you spend less now while spending more in the long run, are dangerous to your financial health. When the financing looks too good to be true, it probably is. In almost every case, you're better off paying cash.

Whether you're buying a mattress, a microwave, or a Maserati, somebody will probably be willing to sell it to you on credit. But the Bible makes it clear that the instant you become a debtor, you also become a servant to the lender (Proverbs 22:7). So do yourself and your family a favor by taking the following simple steps:

1. Pay your credit card balances off every month. If you can't manage to pay off all your balances when they come due, put your credit cards in a drawer and don't use them again until you've paid them off completely.

2. Never buy consumer goods such as clothes, furniture or electronics on credit. Even if the interest rate seems incredibly attractive, don't sign your name on the dotted line; wait until you can afford to pay cash.

3. Don't rent consumer goods or electronics on "rent-to-own" plans. These plans may sound good, but they aren't.

4. If you absolutely must borrow money to purchase a car, buy a good, safe, inexpensive used car that you can pay off in a hurry. It's better to drive a clunker with a small note than a luxury car that's "loaded" with debt.

To sum it up, debt has a few good uses and many bad ones. So beware. And if you're trying to decide whether or not to make that next big purchase, remember that when it comes to borrowed money, less is usually more . . . much more.

A MORTGAGE ON YOUR HOME IS OKAY . . . WITHIN REASON

Unless you were born with a substantial trust fund—and if you were, you're probably not reading this book—you will need to borrow money to purchase your home. And, because home ownership has many benefits, you're probably wise to do so if you use common sense. Don't try to "max out" your mortgage by borrowing every penny that you can. And don't load yourself down with a second mortgage that can further crimp your financial style. Instead, wait until you have saved enough money to make a substantial down payment, and don't buy a more expensive home than you can afford.

TODAY'S TIP FOR HANDLING TOUGH TIMES

Excessive debt—especially credit-card debt used to purchase consumer items—is dangerous to your financial health. So if you want to overcome your financial challenges, you must understand how to manage and eliminate debt.

MORE FROM GOD'S WORD ABOUT
BORROWING MONEY

My child, if you co-sign a loan for a friend or guarantee the debt of someone you hardly know, if you have trapped yourself by your agreement and are caught by what you said, quick, get out of it if you possibly can! You have placed yourself at your friend's mercy. Now swallow your pride; go and beg to have your name erased. Don't put it off. Do it now! Don't rest until you do. Save yourself like a deer escaping from a hunter, like a bird fleeing from a net.

Proverbs 6:1-5 NLT

You can't worship two gods at once. Loving one god, you'll end up hating the other. Adoration of one feeds contempt for the other. You can't worship God and Money both.

Matthew 6:24 MSG

Keep your lives free from the love of money, and be satisfied with what you have.

Hebrews 13:5 NCV

For the love of money is a root of all sorts of evil, and some by longing for it have wandered away from the faith and pierced themselves with many griefs.

1 Timothy 6:10 NASB

MORE POWERFUL IDEAS ABOUT DEBT

Having money may not make people happy, but owing money is sure to make them miserable.

John Maxwell

Getting out of the pit requires we surround ourselves with people who love us enough to support us and lift us up when we are at our ugliest.

Dave Ramsey

God says that when you borrow, you become a servant of the lender; the lender is established as an authority over the borrower. (Proverbs 22:7)

Larry Burkett

It is better to go to bed supperless than rise in debt.

Ben Franklin

Debt is like any other trap. It is easy enough to get into but hard enough to get out of.

Josh Billings

Make up your mind to associate with people who will not pressure you to spend money you don't have for things you don't need.

Marie T. Freeman

QUESTIONS TO CONSIDER

On the lines below, make notes to yourself about your current level of debt. Do you wish you owed less? Are you trying to decrease debt without much success? If so, jot down at least three steps that you can take today to begin paying off your obligations more quickly.

_____

_____

_____

_____

_____

_____

_____

_____

A PRAYER FOR TODAY

Dear Lord, the Bible teaches us that the debtor is servant to the lender. So today and every day, I will think carefully—and prayerfully—before I commit myself to future obligations. Instead of borrowing from the future, I will save for the future. And as each day unfolds, I will strive to walk in Christ's footsteps. Then, when I have done my best to honor Your Word and follow Your Son, I will leave everything else up to You. Amen

Day 18

LEARN FROM
YOUR MISTAKES

The one who conceals his sins will not prosper,
but whoever confesses and renounces them will find mercy.
Proverbs 28:13 HCSB

THE FOCUS FOR TODAY

God is able to take mistakes, when they are
committed to Him, and make of them something
for our good and for His glory.
Ruth Bell Graham

Are you one of those people who has, at one time or another, made a mess of your financial affairs? If so, welcome to a very large club! Almost everyone experiences financial pressures from time to time, and so, perhaps, will you.

Winston Churchill once observed, "Success is going from failure to failure without loss of enthusiasm." What was good for Churchill is also good for you, too. As you live and learn about life, you should expect to make mistakes—and a few financial blunders, too—but you should not allow those missteps to rob you of the enthusiasm you need to fulfill God's plan for your life.

We are imperfect people living in an imperfect world; mistakes are simply part of the price we pay for being here. But, even though mistakes are an inevitable part of life's journey, repeated mistakes should not be. When we commit the inevitable missteps of life, we must correct them, learn from them, and pray for the wisdom not to repeat them. When we do, our mistakes become lessons, and our lives become adventures in growth, not stagnation.

Have you made a financial foul-up or two? You probably have. But here's the big question: Have you used your mistakes as stumbling blocks or stepping stones? The answer to that question will determine how quickly you gain financial security and peace of mind.

LEARN FROM YOUR EXPERIENCES . . . AND USE THEM

Perhaps tough times have turned your world upside down. Maybe it seems to you as if everything in your life has been rearranged. Or perhaps your relationships and your responsibilities have been permanently altered. If so, you may come face to face with the daunting task of finding new purpose for your life. And God is willing to help.

God has an important plan for your life, and part of His plan may well be related to the tough times you're experiencing. After all, you've learned important, albeit hard earned, lessons. And you're certainly wiser today than you were yesterday. So your suffering carries with it great potential: the potential for intense personal growth and the potential to help others.

As you begin to reorganize your life, look for ways to use your experiences for the betterment of others. When you do, you can rest assured that the course of your recovery will depend upon how quickly you discover new people to help and new reasons to live. And as you move through and beyond your own particular tough times, be mindful of this fact: As a survivor, you will have countless opportunities to serve others. By serving others, you will bring glory to God and meaning to the hardships you've endured.

TODAY'S TIP FOR HANDLING TOUGH TIMES

Have you experienced a setback? If so, look for the lesson that God is trying to teach you. Instead of complaining about life's sad state of affairs, learn what needs to be learned, change what needs to be changed, and move on. View failure as an opportunity to reassess God's will for your life. View life's inevitable disappointments as opportunities to learn more about yourself and your world. Life can be difficult at times. And everybody makes mistakes. Your job is to make them only once.

MORE FROM GOD'S WORD ABOUT
GOD'S FORGIVENESS

All the prophets testify about Him that through His name everyone who believes in Him will receive forgiveness of sins.

Acts 10:43 HCSB

When Jesus stood up, He said to her, "Woman, where are they? Has no one condemned you?" "No one, Lord," she answered. "Neither do I condemn you," said Jesus. "Go, and from now on do not sin any more."

John 8:10-11 HCSB

MORE POWERFUL IDEAS ABOUT MISTAKES

One of the ways God refills us after failure is through the blessing of Christian fellowship. Just experiencing the joy of simple activities shared with other children of God can have a healing effect on us.

Anne Graham Lotz

Mistakes offer the possibility for redemption and a new start in God's kingdom. No matter what you're guilty of, God can restore your innocence.

Barbara Johnson

In essence, my testimony is that there is life after failure: abundant, effective, spirit-filled life for those who are willing to repent hard and work hard.

Beth Moore

As you place yourself under the sovereign lordship of Jesus Christ, each mistake or failure can lead you right back to the throne.

Barbara Johnson

Lord, when we are wrong, make us willing to change; and when we are right, make us easy to live with.

Peter Marshall

QUESTIONS TO CONSIDER

In the space below, make a list of at least five of the most important lessons you've learned from your mistakes.

_____

_____

_____

_____

_____

_____

_____

_____

_____

_____

_____

_____

_____

_____

_____

A PRAYER FOR TODAY

*Dear Lord, there's a right way to do things and a wrong
way to do things. When I do things that are wrong,
help me be quick to ask for forgiveness . . .
and quick to correct my mistakes. Amen*

DEFEATING PROCRASTINATION

If you wait for perfect conditions,
you will never get anything done.
Ecclesiastes 11:4 NLT

THE FOCUS FOR TODAY

Not now becomes never.
Martin Luther

When tough economic times arrive, it's easy (and tempting) to avoid those hard-to-do tasks that you would prefer to avoid altogether. Sometimes, fretting seems easier than fixing. But the habit of procrastination takes a double toll: First, important work goes unfinished, and second, valuable energy is wasted in the process of putting off the things that remain undone.

God has created a world that punishes procrastinators and rewards men and women who "do it now." In other words, life doesn't procrastinate. Neither should you. So if you've been putting things off instead of getting things done, here are some things you can do:

1. Have a clear understanding of your short and long term goals, and set your priorities in accordance with those goals.

2. When faced with distasteful tasks, do them immediately, preferably first thing in the morning (even if the unpleasantness is a low-priority activity, go ahead and get it out of the way if it can be completed quickly). Dispatching distasteful tasks sooner rather than later will improve the quality of your day and prevent you from wasting untold amounts of energy in the process of fighting against yourself.

3. Avoid the trap of perfectionism. Be willing to do your best, and be satisfied with the results.

4. If you don't already own one, purchase a daily or weekly planning system that fits your needs. If used properly, a planning calendar is worth many times what you pay for it.

5. Start each work day with a clear written "to-do" list, ranked according to importance. At lunch time, take a moment to collect your thoughts, reexamine your list, and refocus your efforts on the most important things you wish to accomplish during the remainder of the day.

TODAY'S TIP FOR HANDLING TOUGH TIMES

The habit of procrastination is often rooted in the fear of failure, the fear of discomfort, or the fear of embarrassment. Your challenge is to confront these fears and defeat them.

MORE FROM GOD'S WORD ABOUT PROCRASTINATION

If you do nothing in a difficult time, your strength is limited.

Proverbs 24:10 HCSB

If you are too lazy to plow in the right season, you will have no food at the harvest.

Proverbs 20:4 NLT

When you make a vow to God, do not delay in fulfilling it. He has no pleasure in fools; fulfill your vow.

Ecclesiastes 5:4 NIV

We can't afford to waste a minute, must not squander these precious daylight hours in frivolity and indulgence, in sleeping around and dissipation, in bickering and grabbing everything in sight. Get out of bed and get dressed! Don't loiter and linger, waiting until the very last minute. Dress yourselves in Christ, and be up and about!

Romans 13:13-14 MSG

Whatever you do, do it enthusiastically, as something done for the Lord and not for men.

Colossians 3:23 HCSB

MORE POWERFUL IDEAS ABOUT
PROCRASTINATION

I've found that the worst thing I can do when it comes to any kind of potential pressure situation is to put off dealing with it.

John Maxwell

Do the unpleasant work first and enjoy the rest of the day.

Marie T. Freeman

I cannot fix what I will not face.

Jim Gallery

Do not build up obstacles in your imagination. Difficulties must be studied and dealt with, but they must not be magnified by fear.

Norman Vincent Peale

Never confuse activity with productivity.

Rick Warren

Do noble things, do not dream them all day long.

Charles Kingsley

QUESTIONS TO CONSIDER

When something needs to be done, do I see the wisdom in doing it sooner rather than later?

_____

_____

Is the fear of failure holding me back?

_____

_____

When faced with an unpleasant job, do I act promptly, or do I increase my misery by procrastinating?

_____

_____

A PRAYER FOR TODAY

*Dear Lord, when I am confronted with things
that need to be done, give me the courage
and the wisdom to do them now, not later.*
Amen

Day 20

PRAY ABOUT YOUR FINANCES

When a believing person prays, great things happen.

James 5:16 NCV

THE FOCUS FOR TODAY

I have found the perfect antidote for fear.
Whenever it sticks up its ugly face,
I clobber it with prayer.

Dale Evans Rogers

re you in the habit of praying about everything, including your finances? Is prayer an integral part of your daily routine, or is it a hit-or-miss activity? Do you "pray without ceasing"—as the Bible clearly instructs in 1 Thessalonians 5:17—or is prayer little more than an afterthought? If you genuinely wish to receive God's blessings, then you must pray constantly . . . and you must never underestimate the power of prayer.

As you contemplate the quality of your prayer life, here are a few things to consider:

1. God hears your prayers and answers them (Jeremiah 29:11-12).

2. God promises that the prayers of righteous men and women can accomplish great things (James 5:16).

3. God invites you to be still and to feel His presence (Psalm 46:10).

So pray. Start praying in the early morning and keep praying until you fall off to sleep at night. Pray about matters great and small; be watchful for the answers that God most assuredly sends your way; and don't be afraid to pray about your financial resources.

If you're uncertain about the ways that you're choosing to spend money, put your credit card back in your wallet until you've had a meaningful conversation with God.

If you're thinking about changing careers, don't make a move until you've talked extensively to your Heavenly Father. If you want to make major changes in the structure of your financial life, ask God for the strength and wisdom to accomplish His plans. In short, pray often about the way that you earn and spend money. When you do, God will speak to you in the quiet corners of your heart, and as you listen and learn, you'll be rewarded.

Daily prayer and meditation is a matter of will and habit. When you organize your day to include quiet moments with God, you'll soon discover that no time is more precious than the silent moments you spend with Him.

The quality of your life is directly effected by the quality of your prayer life. So do yourself a favor: instead of turning things over in your mind, turn them over to God in prayer. Instead of worrying about your next financial decision, ask God to lead the way. Don't limit your prayers to meals or to bedtime. Pray constantly because God is listening—and He wants to hear from you. And without question, you need to hear from Him.

GOT QUESTIONS?

You've got questions? God's got answers. And if you'd like to hear from Him, here's precisely what you must do: petition Him with a sincere heart; be still; be patient; and listen. Then, in His own time and in His own fashion, God will answer your questions and give you guidance for the journey ahead.

Today, turn over everything to your Creator. Pray constantly about matters great and small. Seek God's instruction and His direction. And remember: God hears your prayers and answers them. But He won't answer the prayers that you don't get around to praying. So pray early and often. And then wait patiently for answers that are sure to come.

TODAY'S TIP FOR HANDLING TOUGH TIMES

Having trouble hearing God? If so, slow yourself down, tune out the distractions, and listen carefully. God has important things to say; your task is to be still and listen.

MORE POWERFUL IDEAS ABOUT PRAYER

We must leave it to God to answer our prayers in His own wisest way. Sometimes, we are so impatient and think that God does not answer. God always answers! He never fails! Be still. Abide in Him.

Mrs. Charles E. Cowman

Learn to pray to God in such a way that you are trusting Him as your Physician to do what He knows is best. Confess to Him the disease, and let Him choose the remedy.

St. Augustine

When you ask God to do something, don't ask timidly; put your whole heart into it.

Marie T. Freeman

Prayer guards hearts and minds and causes God to bring peace out of chaos.

Beth Moore

Are you weak? Weary? Confused? Troubled? Pressured? How is your relationship with God? Is it held in its place of priority? I believe the greater the pressure, the greater your need for time alone with Him.

Kay Arthur

QUESTIONS TO CONSIDER

Things to Pray About: On the lines below, list specific aspects of your financial life that you need to pray about. This list might also include such things as your career, your future, your finances, your spending habits, or the general direction of your life.

_____

_____

_____

_____

_____

_____

_____

_____

_____

_____

A PRAYER FOR TODAY

Dear God, sometimes this world can be a puzzling place. When I am unsure of my next step, keep me aware that You are always near. Give me faith, Father, and let me remember that with Your love and Your power, I can live courageously and faithfully today and every day. Amen

Day 21

SELF-ESTEEM ACCORDING TO GOD

For you made us only a little lower than God,
and you crowned us with glory and honor.

Psalm 8:5 NLT

THE FOCUS FOR TODAY

Your self worth is more important
than your net worth.

Anonymous

When you encounter tough economic times, you may lose self-confidence. Or you may become so focused on what other people are thinking—or saying—that you fail to focus on God. To do so is a mistake of major proportions—don't make it. Instead, seek God's guidance as you focus your energies on becoming the best you that you can possibly be. And when it comes to matters of self-esteem and self-image, seek approval not from your peers, but from your Creator.

Millions of words have been written about various ways to improve self-image and increase self-esteem. Yet, maintaining a healthy self-image is, to a surprising extent, a matter of doing three things: 1. Obeying God 2. Thinking healthy thoughts 3. Finding a purpose for your life that pleases your Creator and yourself. The following common-sense, Biblically-based tips can help you build the kind of self-image—and the kind of life—that both you and God can be proud of:

1. Do the right thing: If you're misbehaving, how can you possibly hope to feel good about yourself? (See Romans 14:12.)

2. Watch what you think: If your inner voice is, in reality, your inner critic, you need to tone down the criticism now. And while you're at it, train yourself to begin thinking thoughts that are more rational, more accepting, and less judgmental. (Philippians 4:8)

3. Spend time with boosters, not critics: Are your friends putting you down? If so, find new friends. (Hebrews 3:13)

4. Don't be a perfectionist: Strive for excellence, but never confuse it with perfection. (Ecclesiastes 11:4, 6)

5. If you're addicted to something unhealthy, stop; if you can't stop, get help: Addictions, of whatever type, create havoc in your life. And disorder. And grief. And low self-esteem. (Exodus 20:3)

6. Find a purpose for your life that is larger than you are: When you're dedicated to something or someone besides yourself, you blossom. (Ephesians 6:7)

7. Don't worry too much about self-esteem: Instead, worry more about living a life that is pleasing to God. Learn to think optimistically. Find a worthy purpose. Find people to love and people to serve. When you do, your self-esteem will, on most days, take care of itself.

TODAY'S TIP FOR HANDLING TOUGH TIMES

Don't make the mistake of selling yourself short. No matter the size of your challenges, you can be sure that you and God, working together, can tackle them.

MORE FROM GOD'S WORD ABOUT
YOUR SELF-WORTH

You're blessed when you're content with just who you are—no more, no less. That's the moment you find yourselves proud owners of everything that can't be bought.

Matthew 5:5 MSG

A devout life does bring wealth, but it's the rich simplicity of being yourself before God.

1 Timothy 6:6 MSG

You made all the delicate, inner parts of my body and knit me together in my mother's womb. Thank you for making me so wonderfully complex! Your workmanship is marvelous—and how well I know it.

Psalm 139:13-14 NLT

My dear children, let's not just talk about love; let's practice real love. This is the only way we'll know we're living truly, living in God's reality. It's also the way to shut down debilitating self-criticism, even when there is something to it. For God is greater than our worried hearts and knows more about us than we do ourselves. And friends, once that's taken care of and we're no longer accusing or condemning ourselves, we're bold and free before God!

1 John 3:18-21 MSG

MORE POWERFUL IDEAS ABOUT
YOUR SELF-WORTH

As you and I lay up for ourselves living, lasting treasures in Heaven, we come to the awesome conclusion that we ourselves are His treasure!

Anne Graham Lotz

The Creator has made us each one of a kind. There is nobody else exactly like us, and there never will be. Each of us is his special creation and is alive for a distinctive purpose.

Luci Swindoll

When it comes to our position before God, we're perfect. When he sees each of us, he sees one who has been made perfect through the One who is perfect—Jesus Christ.

Max Lucado

Give yourself a gift today: be present with yourself. God is. Enjoy your own personality. God does.

Barbara Johnson

Being loved by Him whose opinion matters most gives us the security to risk loving, too—even loving ourselves.

Gloria Gaither

QUESTIONS TO CONSIDER

Do I pay careful attention to the messages that I'm sending myself about myself?

_____

_____

Am I sometimes my own worst critic, and is the criticism really deserved?

_____

_____

Do I remind myself that God loves me . . . and that I should, too?

_____

_____

A PRAYER FOR TODAY

Dear Lord, help me speak courteously to everyone, including myself. And when I make a mistake, help me to forgive myself quickly and thoroughly, just as I forgive others. Amen

Remember That No Problem Is Too Big for God

Is anything too hard for the LORD?

Genesis 18:14 KJV

The Focus for Today

The grace of God is sufficient for all our needs,
for every problem and for every difficulty,
for every broken heart, and for every human sorrow.

Peter Marshall

Here's a riddle: What is it that is too unimportant to pray about, yet too big for God to handle? The answer, of course, is: "nothing." Yet sometimes, when the challenges of the day seem overwhelming, we may spend more time worrying about our troubles than praying about them. And, we may spend more time fretting about our problems than solving them. A far better strategy, of course, is to pray as if everything depended entirely upon God and to work as if everything depended entirely upon us.

Life is an exercise in problem-solving. The question is not whether we will encounter problems; the real question is how we will choose to address them. When it comes to solving the problems of everyday living, we often know precisely what needs to be done, but we may be slow in doing it—especially if what needs to be done is difficult or uncomfortable for us. So we put off till tomorrow what should be done today.

The words of Psalm 34 remind us that the Lord solves problems for "people who do what is right." And usually, "doing what is right" means doing the uncomfortable work of confronting our problems sooner rather than later. So with no further ado, let the problem-solving begin . . . now!

Do Something Today

Perhaps your troubles are simply too big to solve in a single sitting. But just because you can't solve everything doesn't mean that you should do nothing. So today, as a favor to yourself and as a way of breaking the bonds of procrastination, do something to make your situation better. Even a small step in the right direction is still a step in the right direction. And a small step is far, far better than no step at all.

Today's Tip for Handling Tough Times

Problem-solving 101: When it comes to solving problems, work beats worry. Remember: It is better to fix than to fret.

MORE FROM GOD'S WORD ABOUT PROBLEM-SOLVING

People who do what is right may have many problems, but the Lord will solve them all.

Psalm 34:19 NCV

For when the way is rough, your patience has a chance to grow. So let it grow, and don't try to squirm out of your problems.

James 1:3-4 TLB

When you go through deep waters and great trouble, I will be with you. When you go through the rivers of difficulty, you will not drown! When you walk through the fire of oppression, you will not be burned up; the flames will not consume you. For I am the Lord, your God . . . .

Isaiah 43:2-3 NLT

Come to me, all you who are weary and burdened, and I will give you rest. Take my yoke upon you and learn from me, for I am gentle and humble in heart, and you will find rest for your souls. For my yoke is easy and my burden is light.

Matthew 11:28-30 NIV

Be of good courage, and he shall strengthen your heart, all ye that hope in the LORD.

Psalm 31:24 KJV

MORE POWERFUL IDEAS ABOUT PROBLEMS

Troubles we bear trustfully can bring us a fresh vision of God and a new outlook on life, an outlook of peace and hope.

Billy Graham

No matter how heavy the burden, daily strength is given, so I expect we need not give ourselves any concern as to what the outcome will be. We must simply go forward.

Annie Armstrong

We must face today as children of tomorrow. We must meet the uncertainties of this world with the certainty of the world to come. To the pure in heart nothing really bad can happen . . . not death, but sin, should be our greatest fear.

A. W. Tozer

Trial and triumph are what God uses to scribble all over the pages of our lives. They are signs that He is using us, loving us, shaping us to His image, enjoying our companionship, delivering us from evil, and writing eternity into our hearts.

Barbara Johnson

QUESTIONS TO CONSIDER

When I encounter difficulties, do I understand the importance of looking for solutions?

_____

_____

Have I formed the habit of tackling problems sooner rather than later?

_____

_____

When I encounter difficulties, do I work to solve the problems instead of worrying about them, or do I often worry more than I work?

_____

_____

A PRAYER FOR TODAY

Lord, sometimes my problems are simply too big for me, but they are never too big for You. Let me turn my troubles over to You, Lord, and let me trust in You today and for all eternity. Amen

Day 23

ACCEPTING ADVICE

*A wise man will hear and increase learning,
and a man of understanding will attain wise counsel.*
Proverbs 1:5 NKJV

THE FOCUS FOR TODAY

It takes a wise person to give good advice,
but an even wiser person to take it.
Marie T. Freeman

If you find yourself caught up in a difficult situation, it's time to start searching for knowledgeable friends and mentors who can give you solid advice. Why do you need help evaluating the person in the mirror? Because you're simply too close to that person, that's why. Sometimes, you'll be tempted to give yourself straight A's when you deserve considerably lower grades. On other occasions, you'll become your own worst critic, giving yourself a string of failing marks when you deserve better. The truth, of course, is often somewhere in the middle.

Finding a wise mentor is only half the battle. It takes just as much wisdom—and sometimes more—to act upon good advice as it does to give it. So find people you can trust, listen to them carefully, and act accordingly.

FIND A MENTOR

If you're going through tough times, it's helpful to find mentors who have been there, and done that—people who have experienced your particular challenge and lived to tell about it.

When you find mentors who are godly men and women, you become a more godly person yourself. That's why you should seek out advisers who, by their words and their presence, make you a better person and a better Christian.

Today, as a gift to yourself, select, from your friends and family members, a mentor whose judgment you trust. Then listen carefully to your mentor's advice and be willing to accept that advice, even if accepting it requires effort, or pain, or both. Consider your mentor to be God's gift to you. Thank God for that gift, and use it for the glory of His kingdom.

TODAY'S TIP FOR HANDLING TOUGH TIMES

If you can't seem to listen to constructive criticism with an open mind, perhaps you've got a severe case of old-fashioned stubbornness. If so, ask God to soften your heart, open your ears, and enlighten your mind.

MORE FROM GOD'S WORD ABOUT
ACCEPTING ADVICE

He is God. Let him do whatever he thinks best.

1 Samuel 3:18 MSG

It is better to be a poor but wise youth than to be an old and foolish king who refuses all advice.

Ecclesiastes 4:13 NLT

It is better to listen to rebuke from a wise person than to listen to the song of fools.

Ecclesiastes 7:5 HCSB

Know-it-alls don't like being told what to do; they avoid the company of wise men and women.

Proverbs 15:12 MSG

Listen to counsel and receive instruction so that you may be wise in later life.

Proverbs 19:20 HCSB

MORE POWERFUL IDEAS ABOUT MENTORS

God guides through the counsel of good people.

E. Stanley Jones

A single word, if spoken in a friendly spirit, may be sufficient to turn one from dangerous error.

Fanny Crosby

No matter how crazy or nutty your life has seemed, God can make something strong and good out of it. He can help you grow wide branches for others to use as shelter.

Barbara Johnson

God often keeps us on the path by guiding us through the counsel of friends and trusted spiritual advisors.

Bill Hybels

Do not open your heart to every man, but discuss your affairs with one who is wise and who fears God.

Thomas à Kempis

Yes, the Spirit was sent to be our Counselor. Yes, Jesus speaks to us personally. But often he works through another human being.

John Eldredge

QUESTIONS TO CONSIDER

Do I understand the importance of finding—and listening to—mentors?

_____

_____

Am I willing to be a mentor to others?

_____

_____

Am I willing to listen carefully to advice and, when appropriate, to take it? Or am I a little too stubborn to take advice from others?

_____

_____

A PRAYER FOR TODAY

Dear Lord, thank You for the mentors whom You have placed along my path. When I am troubled, let me turn to them for help, for guidance, for comfort, and for perspective. And Father, let me be a friend and mentor to others, so that my love for You may be demonstrated by my genuine concern for them. Amen

FAITH MOVES MOUNTAINS

For whatever is born of God overcomes the world.
And this is the victory that has
overcome the world—our faith.

1 John 5:4 NKJV

THE FOCUS FOR TODAY

Trials are not enemies of faith but opportunities
to reveal God's faithfulness.

Barbara Johnson

Every life—including yours—is a grand adventure made great by faith. Every step of the way, through every triumph and tragedy, God will stand by your side and strengthen you . . . if you have faith in Him.

Job had every opportunity to give up on himself and to give up on God. But despite his suffering, Job refused to curse His Creator. Job trusted God in the darkest moments of his life, and so did Jesus.

Before His crucifixion, Jesus went to the Mount of Olives and poured out His heart to God (Luke 22). Jesus knew of the agony that He was destined to endure, but He also knew that God's will must be done. We, like our Savior, face trials that bring fear and trembling to the very depths of our souls, but like Jesus, we should seek God's will, not our own.

When you entrust your life to God completely and without reservation, He will give you the strength to meet any challenge, the courage to face any trial, and the wisdom to live in His righteousness and in His peace. So strengthen your faith through praise, through worship, through Bible study, and through prayer. And trust God's plans. With Him, all things are possible, and He stands ready to open a world of possibilities to you . . . if you have faith.

NOURISH YOUR FAITH

When we trust God, we should trust Him without reservation. But sometimes, especially during life's darker days, trusting God may be difficult. Yet this much is certain: whatever our circumstances, we must continue to plant the seeds of faith in our hearts, trusting that in time God will bring forth a bountiful harvest. Planting the seeds for that harvest requires work, which is perfectly okay with God. After all, He never gives us burdens that we cannot bear.

It is important to remember that the work required to build and sustain our faith is an ongoing process. Corrie ten Boom advised, "Be filled with the Holy Spirit; join a church where the members believe the Bible and know the Lord; seek the fellowship of other Christians; learn and be nourished by God's Word and His many promises. Conversion is not the end of your journey—it is only the beginning."

The work of nourishing your faith can and should be joyful work. The hours that you invest in Bible study, prayer, meditation, and worship should be times of enrichment and celebration. And, as you continue to build your life upon a foundation of faith, you will discover that the journey toward spiritual maturity lasts a lifetime. As a child of God, you are never fully "grown": instead, you can continue "growing up" every day of your life. And that's exactly what God wants you to do.

TODAY'S TIP FOR HANDLING TOUGH TIMES

Feelings come and feelings go, but God never changes. So when you have a choice between trusting your feelings or trusting God, trust God. And remember that if your faith is strong enough, you and God—working together—can move mountains.

MORE FROM GOD'S WORD ABOUT FAITH

Be on the alert, stand firm in the faith, act like men, be strong.

1 Corinthians 16:13 NASB

It is impossible to please God apart from faith. And why? Because anyone who wants to approach God must believe both that he exists and that he cares enough to respond to those who seek him.

Hebrews 11:6 MSG

Fight the good fight of faith; take hold of the eternal life to which you were called....

1 Timothy 6:12 NASB

MORE POWERFUL IDEAS ABOUT FAITH

It may be the most difficult time of your life. You may be enduring your own whirlwind. But the whirlwind is a temporary experience. Your faithful, caring Lord will see you through.

Charles Swindoll

I am truly grateful that faith enables me to move past the question of "Why?"

Zig Ziglar

When you enroll in the "school of faith," you never know what may happen next. The life of faith presents challenges that keep you going—and keep you growing!

Warren Wiersbe

Nothing is more disastrous than to study faith, analyze faith, make noble resolves of faith, but never actually to make the leap of faith.

Vance Havner

Faith is our spiritual oxygen. It not only keeps us alive in God, but enables us to grow stronger....

Joyce Landorf Heatherly

QUESTIONS TO CONSIDER

Am I willing to ask God to become a full partner in my life?

_____

_____

Am I willing to pray as if everything depended upon God and work as if everything depended upon me?

_____

_____

After I've done my best, am I willing to trust God's plan and His timetable for my life?

_____

_____

A PRAYER FOR TODAY

Lord, sometimes this world is a terrifying place.
When I am filled with uncertainty and doubt,
give me faith. In life's dark moments,
help me remember that You are always near and
that You can overcome any challenge. Today, Lord,
and forever, I will place my trust in You. Amen

Day 25

LIVE COURAGEOUSLY

*They do not fear bad news; they confidently trust the Lord
to care for them. They are confident and fearless
and can face their foes triumphantly.*

Psalm 112:7-8 NLT

THE FOCUS FOR TODAY

Faith not only can help you through a crisis,
it can help you to approach life after the hard times
with a whole new perspective. It can help you
adopt an outlook of hope and courage
through faith to face reality.

John Maxwell

Every person's life is a tapestry of events: some wonderful, some not-so-wonderful, and some downright disastrous. When we visit the mountaintops of life, praising God isn't hard—in fact, it's easy. In our moments of triumph, we can bow our heads and thank God for our victories. But when we fail to reach the mountaintops, when we endure the inevitable losses that are a part of every person's life, we find it much tougher to give God the praise He deserves. Yet wherever we find ourselves, whether on the mountaintops of life or in life's darkest valleys, we must still offer thanks to God, giving thanks in all circumstances.

The next time you find yourself worried about the challenges of today or the uncertainties of tomorrow, ask yourself this question: are you really ready to place your concerns and your life in God's all-powerful, all-knowing, all-loving hands? If the answer to that question is yes—as it should be—then you can draw courage today from the source of strength that never fails: your Father in heaven.

God is not a distant being. He is not absent from our world, nor is He absent from your world. God is not "out there"; He is "right here," continuously reshaping His universe, and continuously reshaping the lives of those who dwell in it.

God is with you always, listening to your thoughts and prayers, watching over your every move. If the demands of everyday life weigh down upon you, you may be tempted to ignore God's presence or—worse yet—to lose faith in His promises. But, when you quiet yourself and acknowledge His presence, God will touch your heart and restore your courage.

At this very moment—as you're fulfilling your obligations and overcoming tough times—God is seeking to work in you and through you. He's asking you to live abundantly and courageously . . . and He's ready to help. So why not let Him do it . . . starting now?

TODAY'S TIP FOR HANDLING TOUGH TIMES

With God as your partner, you have nothing to fear. Why? Because you and God, working together, can handle absolutely anything that comes your way. So the next time you'd like an extra measure of courage, recommit yourself to a true one-on-one relationship with your Creator. When you sincerely turn to Him, He will never fail you.

MORE FROM GOD'S WORD ABOUT COURAGE

Be strong and courageous, and do the work. Don't be afraid or discouraged by the size of the task, for the LORD God, my God, is with you. He will not fail you or forsake you.

1 Chronicles 28:20 NLT

Therefore, being always of good courage . . . we walk by faith, not by sight.

2 Corinthians 5:6-7 NASB

God doesn't want us to be shy with his gifts, but bold and loving and sensible.

2 Timothy 1:7 MSG

The LORD himself goes before you and will be with you; he will never leave you nor forsake you. Do not be afraid; do not be discouraged.

Deuteronomy 31:8 NIV

But Moses said to the people, "Do not fear! Stand by and see the salvation of the LORD.

Exodus 14:13 NASB

MORE POWERFUL IDEAS ABOUT COURAGE

Seeing that a pilot steers the ship in which we sail, who will never allow us to perish even in the midst of shipwrecks, there is no reason why our minds should be overwhelmed with fear and overcome with weariness.

John Calvin

Like dynamite, God's power is only latent power until it is released. You can release God's dynamite power into people's lives and into the world through faith, through words, and through prayer.

Bill Bright

Faith is stronger than fear.

John Maxwell

Do not let Satan deceive you into being afraid of God's plans for your life.

R. A. Torrey

Jesus Christ can make the weakest man into a divine dreadnought, fearing nothing.

Oswald Chambers

Perhaps I am stronger than I think.

Thomas Merton

QUESTIONS TO CONSIDER

Do I consider God to be my partner in every aspect of my life?

_____

_____

Do I trust God to handle the problems that are simply too big for me to solve?

_____

_____

Am I really willing to place the future—and my future—in God's hands?

_____

_____

A PRAYER FOR TODAY

*Lord, sometimes I face challenges that leave me
breathless. When I am fearful, let me lean upon You.
Keep me ever mindful, Lord, that You are my God,
my strength, and my shield. With You by my side,
I have nothing to fear. And, with Your Son Jesus as my
Savior, I have received the priceless gift of eternal life.
Help me to be a grateful and courageous servant
this day and every day. Amen*

ARE YOU TOO FOCUSED ON POSSESSIONS?

Don't collect for yourselves treasures on earth, where moth and rust destroy and where thieves break in and steal. But collect for yourselves treasures in heaven, where neither moth nor rust destroys, and where thieves don't break in and steal. For where your treasure is, there your heart will be also.

Matthew 6:19-21 HCSB

THE FOCUS FOR TODAY

True contentment comes from godliness in the heart, not from wealth in the hand.

Warren Wiersbe

All too often we focus our thoughts and energies on the accumulation of earthly treasures, creating untold stress in our lives and leaving precious little time to accumulate the only treasures that really matter: the spiritual kind. Our material possessions have the potential to do great good—depending upon how we use them. If we allow the things we own to own us, we may pay dearly for our misplaced priorities.

Society focuses intently on material possessions, but God's Word teaches us time and again that money matters little when compared to the spiritual gifts that the Creator offers to those who put Him first in their lives. So today, keep your possessions in perspective. Remember that God should come first, and everything else next. When you give God His rightful place in your heart, you'll have a clearer vision of the things that really matter. Then, you can joyfully thank your Heavenly Father for spiritual blessings that are, in truth, too numerous to count.

OUR REAL RICHES

How important are your material possessions? Not as important as you might think. In the life of a committed Christian, material possessions should play a rather small role. In fact, when we become overly enamored with the things we own, we needlessly distance ourselves from the peace that God offers to those who place Him at the center of their lives.

Of course, we all need the basic necessities of life, but once we meet those needs for ourselves and for our families, the piling up of possessions creates more problems than it solves. Our real riches, of course, are not of this world. We are never really rich until we are rich in spirit.

Do you find yourself wrapped up in the concerns of the material world? If so, it's time to reorder your priorities by turning your thoughts and your prayers to more important matters. And, it's time to begin storing up riches that will endure throughout eternity: the spiritual kind.

TODAY'S TIP FOR HANDLING TOUGH TIMES

The world wants you to believe that money and possessions can buy happiness. Don't believe it! Genuine happiness comes not from money, but from the things that money can't buy—starting, of course, with your relationship to God and His only begotten Son.

MORE FROM GOD'S WORD ABOUT MATERIALISM

Do not love the world or the things in the world. If anyone loves the world, the love of the Father is not in him.

1 John 2:15 NKJV

He who trusts in his riches will fall, but the righteous will flourish . . . .

Proverbs 11:28 NKJV

For what will it profit a man if he gains the whole world, and loses his own soul? Or what will a man give in exchange for his soul?

Mark 8:36-37 NKJV

For where your treasure is, there your heart will be also.

Luke 12:34 NKJV

Since we entered the world penniless and will leave it penniless, if we have bread on the table and shoes on our feet, that's enough.

1 Timothy 6:7-8 MSG

MORE POWERFUL IDEAS ABOUT MATERIALISM

The socially prescribed affluent, middle-class lifestyle has become so normative in our churches that we discern little conflict between it and the Christian lifestyle prescribed in the New Testament.

Tony Campolo

We are made spiritually lethargic by a steady diet of materialism.

Mary Morrison Suggs

Greed is enslaving. The more you have, the more you want—until eventually avarice consumes you.

Kay Arthur

Here's a simple test: If you can see it, it's not going to last. The things that last are the things you cannot see.

Dennis Swanberg

The cross is laid on every Christian. It begins with the call to abandon the attachments of this world.

Dietrich Bonhoeffer

QUESTIONS TO CONSIDER

Do I genuinely understand that material possessions will not bring me lasting happiness?

_____

_____

Do I understand that my possessions are actually God's possessions, and do I use those possessions for His purposes?

_____

_____

Do my spending habits reflect the values that I hold most dear, and am I a faithful steward of my resources?

_____

_____

A PRAYER FOR TODAY

*Heavenly Father, when I focus intently upon You,
I am blessed. When I focus too intently on material
possessions, I am troubled. Make my priorities
pleasing to You, Father, and make me
a worthy servant of Your Son. Amen*

DON'T STOP GIVING TO GOD

Every tenth of the land's produce,
grain from the soil or fruit from the trees,
belongs to the Lord; it is holy to the Lord.

Leviticus 27:30 HCSB

THE FOCUS FOR TODAY

For many of us, the great obstacle to charity
lies not in our luxurious living or desire for more money,
but in our fear of insecurity.

C. S. Lewis

In Leviticus, we receive clear instructions from our Lord: One tenth of our production, of whatever type, belongs to Him. Period. When we offer a tenth of our earnings to God, we are blessed in the knowledge that we have obeyed His Holy Word. But, when we fail to offer Him the firstfruits of our labors, we live in rebellion against God's will for our lives.

Everything that we possess is a gift from our Creator. Our tithes are a tangible demonstration of our gratitude to Him. To withhold the tithe is to disobey the One who sent His Son to die on a cross for each of us.

We should never think of our tithes as gifts to God. They are, instead, a return to Him of that which is already His. God is all-powerful; He uses our offerings to accomplish His purposes, but He does not need them. We, on the other hand, desperately need the experience of tithing to Him. We need the assurance and peace that result from obedience to our Creator.

We must tithe, first and foremost, because God has commanded us to do so. When we do, we will surely experience the abundance that accompanies a life of obedience to Him.

Do you seek God's abundance and His peace? Then share the blessings that God has given you. Share your possessions, share your faith, share your testimony, and share your love. God expects no less; He deserves no less; and neither, come to think of it, do your neighbors.

Today, you may feel the urge to hoard your blessings. Don't do it. Instead, give generously to your neighbors, and do so without fanfare. Find a need and fill it . . . humbly. Lend a helping hand and share a word of kindness . . . anonymously. This is God's way.

TODAY'S TIP FOR HANDLING TOUGH TIMES

When times are tough, you may be tempted to give God less than He deserves. Don't do it! God doesn't ask for much (only 10%). And you owe it to Him—and to yourself—to give Him what He deserves.

MORE FROM GOD'S WORD ABOUT GENEROSITY

So let each one give as he purposes in his heart, not grudgingly or of necessity; for God loves a cheerful giver.

2 Corinthians 9:7 NKJV

In every way I've shown you that by laboring like this, it is necessary to help the weak and to keep in mind the words of the Lord Jesus, for He said, "It is more blessed to give than to receive."

Acts 20:35 HCSB

Dear friend, you are showing your faith by whatever you do for the brothers, and this you are doing for strangers.

3 John 1:5 HCSB

Bear one another's burdens, and so fulfill the law of Christ.

Galatians 6:2 NKJV

If a brother or sister is without clothes and lacks daily food, and one of you says to them, "Go in peace, keep warm, and eat well," but you don't give them what the body needs, what good is it?

James 2:15–16 HCSB

MORE POWERFUL IDEAS ABOUT GENEROSITY

We hurt people by being too busy, too busy to notice their needs.

Billy Graham

It is one of the most beautiful compensations of life that no one can sincerely try to help another without helping herself.

Barbara Johnson

Make it a rule, and pray to God to help you to keep it, never, if possible, to lie down at night without being able to say: "I have made one human being at least a little wiser, or a little happier, or at least a little better this day."

Charles Kingsley

When you add value to others, you do not take anything away from yourself.

John Maxwell

Fragile and delicate are the feelings of most who seek our help. They need to sense we are there because we care . . . not just because it's our job.

Charles Swindoll

QUESTIONS TO CONSIDER

When I have questions about the level of my giving, am I willing to ask God for guidance?

_____

_____

Do I clearly understand that God has commanded me to be generous?

_____

_____

Do I believe that when I obey God's commandments, that I will be blessed because of my obedience?

_____

_____

A PRAYER FOR TODAY

Lord, during good times and during hard times, make me a generous and cheerful giver. Help me to give generously of my time and my possessions as I care for those in need. And, make me a humble giver, Lord, so that all the glory and the praise might be Yours.
Amen

Day 28

Time for Renewal

I will give you a new heart and put a new spirit within you.
Ezekiel 36:26 HCSB

The Focus for Today

God specializes in things fresh and firsthand.
His plans for you this year may outshine those of the past.
He's prepared to fill your days with reasons
to give Him praise.

Joni Eareckson Tada

On occasion, the demands of daily life can drain us of our strength and rob us of the joy that is rightfully ours in Christ. When we find ourselves tired, discouraged, or worse, there is a source from which we can draw the power needed to recharge our spiritual batteries. That source is God.

Is your spiritual battery running low? Is your energy on the wane? Are your emotions frayed? If so, it's time to turn your thoughts and your prayers to your Heavenly Father. When you do, He will provide for Your needs, and He will restore your soul.

UNDERSTANDING DEPRESSION

Throughout our lives, all of us must endure personal losses that leave us struggling to find hope. The sadness that accompanies such losses is an inescapable fact of life—but in time, we move beyond our grief as the sadness runs its course and life returns to normal. Depression, however, is more than sadness . . . much more.

Depression is a physical and emotional condition that is, in almost all cases, treatable with medication and counseling. And it is not a disease to be taken lightly. Left untreated, depression presents real dangers to patients' physical health and to their emotional wellbeing.

If you're feeling blue, perhaps it's a logical response to the disappointments of everyday life. But if your feelings of sadness have lasted longer than you think they should—or if someone close to you fears that your sadness may have evolved into clinical depression—it's time to seek professional help.

Here are a few simple guidelines to consider as you make decisions about possible medical treatment:

1. If your feelings of sadness have resulted in persistent and prolonged changes in sleep patterns, or if you've experienced a significant change in weight (either gain or loss), consult your physician.

2. If you have persistent urges toward self-destructive behavior, or if you feel as though you have lost the will to live, consult a professional counselor or physician immediately.

3. If someone you trust urges you to seek counseling, schedule a session with a professionally trained counselor to evaluate your condition.

4. If you are plagued by consistent, prolonged, severe feelings of hopelessness, consult a physician, a professional counselor, or your pastor.

God's Word has much to say about every aspect of your life, including your emotional health. And, when you face concerns of any sort—including symptoms of depression—remember that God is with You. Your Creator Father intends that His joy should become your joy. Yet sometimes, amid the inevitable hustle and bustle of life, you may forfeit—albeit temporarily—God's joy as you wrestle with the challenges of daily living.

So, if you're feeling genuinely depressed, trust your medical doctor to do his or her part. Then, place your ultimate trust in your benevolent Heavenly Father. His healing touch, like His love, endures forever.

TODAY'S TIP FOR HANDLING TOUGH TIMES

God wants to give you peace, and He wants to renew your spirit. It's up to you to slow down and give Him a chance to do so.

MORE FROM GOD'S WORD ABOUT RENEWAL

The One who was sitting on the throne said, "Look! I am making everything new!" Then he said, "Write this, because these words are true and can be trusted."

Revelation 21:5 NCV

When doubts filled my mind, your comfort gave me renewed hope and cheer.

Psalm 94:19 NLT

Create in me a pure heart, O God, and renew a steadfast spirit within me. Do not cast me from your presence or take your Holy Spirit from me. Restore to me the joy of your salvation and grant me a willing spirit, to sustain me.

Psalm 51:10-12 NIV

He makes me to lie down in green pastures; He leads me beside the still waters. He restores my soul; He leads me in the paths of righteousness For His name's sake.

Psalm 23:2–3 NKJV

Come to Me, all you who labor and are heavy laden, and I will give you rest. Take My yoke upon you and learn from Me, for I am gentle and lowly in heart, and you will find rest for your souls. For My yoke is easy and My burden is light.

Matthew 11:28-30 NKJV

QUESTIONS TO CONSIDER

Do I believe that God can make all things new—including me?

_____

_____

Do I take time each day to be still and let God give me perspective and direction?

_____

_____

Do I understand the importance of getting a good night's sleep?

_____

_____

A PRAYER FOR TODAY

Lord, You are my rock and my strength. When I grow weary, let me turn my thoughts and my prayers to You. When I am discouraged, restore my faith in You. Let me always trust in Your promises, Lord, and let me draw strength from those promises and from Your unending love. Amen

A RENEWED SENSE OF PURPOSE

You will show me the way of life,
granting me the joy of your presence
and the pleasures of living with you forever.

Psalm 16:11 NLT

THE FOCUS FOR TODAY

We should not be upset when unexpected and upsetting
things happen. God, in His wisdom, means to make
something of us which we have not yet attained,
and He is dealing with us accordingly.

J. I. Packer

If you're experiencing financial challenges, you may be asking yourself "What does God want me to do next?" Perhaps you're pondering your future, uncertain of your plans, unsure of your next step. But even if you don't have a clear plan for the next step of your life's journey, you may rest assured that God does.

God has a plan for the universe, and He has a plan for you. He understands that plan as thoroughly and completely as He knows you. If you seek God's will earnestly and prayerfully, He will make His plans known to you in His own time and in His own way.

Do you sincerely want to discover God's purpose for your life? If so, you must first be willing to live in accordance with His commandments. You must also study God's Word and be watchful for His signs. Finally, you should open yourself up to the Creator every day—beginning with this one—and you must have faith that He will soon reveal His plans to you.

Perhaps your vision of God's purpose for your life has been clouded by a wish list that you have expected God to dutifully fulfill. Perhaps, you have fervently hoped that God would create a world that unfolds according to your wishes, not His. If so, you have probably experienced more disappointment than satisfaction and more frustration than peace. A better strategy is to conform your will to

God's (and not to struggle vainly in an attempt to conform His will to yours).

Sometimes, God's plans and purposes may seem unmistakably clear to you. If so, push ahead. But other times, He may lead you through the wilderness before He directs you to the Promised Land. So be patient and keep seeking His will for your life. When you do, you'll be amazed at the marvelous things that an all-powerful, all-knowing God can do.

YOUR FUTURE ACCORDING TO GOD

Because we are saved by a risen Christ, we can have hope for the future, no matter how troublesome our present circumstances may seem. After all, God has promised that we are His throughout eternity. And, He has told us that we must place our hopes in Him.

Of course, we will face disappointments and failures while we are here on earth, but these are only temporary defeats. Of course, this world can be a place of trials and tribulations, but when we place our trust in the Giver of all things good, we are secure. God has promised us peace, joy, and eternal life. And God keeps His promises today, tomorrow, and forever.

Are you willing to place your future in the hands of a loving and all-knowing God? Do you trust in the ultimate goodness of His plan for your life? Will you face today's challenges with optimism and hope? You should. After all, God created you for a very important purpose: His purpose. And you still have important work to do: His work.

Today, as you live in the present and look to the future, remember that God has a plan for you. Act—and believe—accordingly.

TODAY'S TIP FOR HANDLING TOUGH TIMES

Perhaps you're in a hurry to understand God's unfolding plan for your life. If so, remember that God operates according to a perfect timetable. That timetable is His, not yours. So be patient. God may have quite a few lessons to teach you before you are fully prepared to do His will and fulfill His purpose.

MORE FROM GOD'S WORD ABOUT PURPOSE

Whatever you do, do all to the glory of God.

1 Corinthians 10:31 NKJV

You're sons of Light, daughters of Day. We live under wide open skies and know where we stand. So let's not sleepwalk through life . . .

1 Thessalonians 5:5-6 MSG

We look at this Son and see the God who cannot be seen. We look at this Son and see God's original purpose in everything created.

Colossians 1:15 MSG

To everything there is a season, a time for every purpose under heaven.

Ecclesiastes 3:1 NKJV

There is one thing I always do. Forgetting the past and straining toward what is ahead, I keep trying to reach the goal and get the prize for which God called me . . . .

Philippians 3:13–14 NCV

QUESTIONS TO CONSIDER

Do I understand the importance of discovering (or rediscovering, if necessary) God's unfolding purpose for my life?

_____

_____

Do I consult God on matters great and small?

_____

_____

Do I pray about my plans for the future, and do I remain open to the opportunities and challenges that God places before me.

_____

_____

A PRAYER FOR TODAY

Dear Lord, let Your purposes be my purposes. Let Your priorities be my priorities. Let Your will be my will. Let Your Word be my guide. And, let me grow in faith and in wisdom today and every day. Amen

Day 30

FOLLOW HIM

*Then Jesus said to His disciples, "If anyone wants to come
with Me, he must deny himself, take up his cross,
and follow Me. For whoever wants to save his life will lose it,
but whoever loses his life because of Me will find it."*

Matthew 16:24-25 HCSB

THE FOCUS FOR TODAY

You who suffer take heart.
Christ is the answer to sorrow.

Billy Graham

J esus walks with you. Are you walking with Him seven days a week, and not just on Sunday mornings? Are you a seven-day-a-week Christian who carries your faith with you to work each day, or do you try to keep Jesus at a "safe" distance when you're not sitting in church? Hopefully, you understand the wisdom of walking with Christ all day, every day.

Jesus loved you so much that He endured unspeakable humiliation and suffering for you. How will you respond to Christ's sacrifice? Will you take up His cross and follow Him—during good times and tough times—or will you choose another path? When you place your hopes squarely at the foot of the cross, when you place Jesus squarely at the center of your life, you will be blessed.

Do you seek to fulfill God's purpose for your life? Do you seek spiritual abundance? Would you like to partake in "the peace that passes all understanding"? Then follow Christ. Follow Him by picking up His cross today and every day that you live. When you do, you will quickly discover that Christ's love has the power to change everything, including you.

YOUR ETERNAL JOURNEY

Eternal life is not an event that begins when you die. Eternal life begins when you invite Jesus into your heart right here on earth. So it's important to remember that God's plans for you are not limited to the ups and downs of everyday life. If you've allowed Jesus to reign over your heart, you've already begun your eternal journey.

Today, give praise to the Creator for His priceless gift, the gift of eternal life. And then, when you've offered Him your thanks and your praise, share His Good News with all who cross your path.

TODAY'S TIP FOR HANDLING TOUGH TIMES

Following Christ is a matter of obedience. If you want to be a little more like Jesus . . . learn about His teachings, follow in His footsteps, and obey His commandments.

MORE FROM GOD'S WORD ABOUT
FOLLOWING CHRIST

Then he told them what they could expect for themselves: "Anyone who intends to come with me has to let me lead."

Luke 9:23 MSG

I've laid down a pattern for you. What I've done, you do.

John 13:15 MSG

No one can serve two masters. Either he will hate the one and love the other, or he will be devoted to the one and despise the other.

Matthew 6:24 NIV

Whoever is not willing to carry the cross and follow me is not worthy of me. Those who try to hold on to their lives will give up true life. Those who give up their lives for me will hold on to true life.

Matthew 10:38-39 NCV

If anyone would come after me, he must deny himself and take up his cross and follow me.

Mark 8:34 NIV

MORE POWERFUL IDEAS ABOUT FOLLOWING CHRIST

Jesus Christ is not a security from storms. He is perfect security in storms.

Kathy Troccoli

In the midst of the pressure and the heat, I am confident His hand is on my life, developing my faith until I display His glory, transforming me into a vessel of honor that pleases Him!

Anne Graham Lotz

Sometimes we get tired of the burdens of life, but we know that Jesus Christ will meet us at the end of life's journey. And, that makes all the difference.

Billy Graham

The Lord gets His best soldiers out of the highlands of affliction.

C. H. Spurgeon

God takes us through struggles and difficulties so that we might become increasingly committed to Him.

Charles Swindoll

QUESTIONS TO CONSIDER

Do I really believe that my relationship with Jesus should be one of servant and Master? And I am behaving like His servant?

_____

_____

Am I attempting to follow in Christ's footsteps, despite my imperfections?

_____

_____

Do I sense a joyful abundance that is mine when I follow Christ?

_____

_____

A PRAYER FOR TODAY

Dear Jesus, because I am Your disciple, I will trust You, I will obey Your teachings, and I will share Your Good News. You have given me life abundant and life eternal, and I will follow You today and forever. Amen

20 FINANCIAL RULES FOR CHRISTIANS

1. Put God First, and Keep Money in Perspective

No servant can serve two masters. Either he will hate the one and love the other, or he will be devoted to the one and despise the other. You cannot serve both God and Money.

Luke 16:13 NIV

As you prioritize matters of importance for you and yours, remember that God is almighty, but the dollar is not. So as you consider ways to achieve financial security, it's wise to place first things first, starting with God.

2. Read the Bible Every Day

Thy word is a lamp unto my feet, and a light unto my path.

Psalm 119:105 KJV

Countless books have been written about money—how to make it and how to keep it. But if you're a Christian, you probably already own at least one copy—and probably several copies—of the world's foremost guide to financial security. That book is the Holy Bible.

God's Word is not only a roadmap to eternal life, but it is also an indispensable guidebook for life here on earth. As such, the Bible has much to say about your life, your faith, and your finances.

3. Keep Improving Your Skills Throughout Your Working Life

When a wise man is instructed, he gains knowledge.

Proverbs 21:11 NIV

If you want to live well and retire before you're too old to enjoy it, you need the ability to create income and keep it. So, if you're making less than you need—or if you earn less than you think you should—put yourself on a steady diet of continuing education, on-the-job training, networking, and general, all-purpose skill building.

In a rapidly changing world, if you're not constantly upgrading your abilities, you're limiting your options, not to mention your income.

4. Find Work You Enjoy and Feel Good About

Do not neglect the gift that is in you.

1 Timothy 4:14 NKJV

If you don't enjoy your work—or if you don't feel good about what you're doing—you probably won't be very good at it. So your challenge is straightforward: First, find a job that you don't dread. Then, keep searching until you find a job that you actually *enjoy* (yes, those kinds of jobs are out there and quite a few people have them).

5. Learn to Spend Less Than You Make

Discipline yourself for the purpose of godliness.

1 Timothy 4:7 NASB

If there's a single, five-word principle for achieving financial security, this is it: "Spend less than you make." This concept is so simple that a child can understand it, yet millions of adults can't seem to get it right. If you're spending everything you make today—or worse yet, borrowing against the future to finance your current lifestyle—you're headed straight for economic quicksand, and fast.

6. Learn to Save

The wise have wealth and luxury, but fools spend whatever they get.

Proverbs 21:20 NLT

Once you've acquired the habit of living at a profit, what should you do with the money that's left over at the end of each month? Well, in the beginning, you should probably get started by socking all of it away in a government-insured bank account. If you work for a salary and receive a regular paycheck, you should be on a regular savings plan that allows you to save (in a separate savings account) from every single paycheck. If your compensation is irregular—for example, if you work on commission—you should establish a sensible savings plan that kicks in whenever you receive a substantial paycheck.

7. Establish Bigger Cash Reserves Than You Think You'll Probably Need

Have them gather all the food and grain of these good years into the royal storehouses, and store it away so there will be food in the cities. That way there will be enough to eat when the seven years of famine come. Otherwise disaster will surely strike the land, and all the people will die.

Genesis 41:35-36 NLT

If you're living on the financial edge, barely making it from paycheck to paycheck, you'll find yourself constantly fretting about your bills: which bills need to be paid today, and which ones can wait until Friday. It's an uncomfortable way to live, and you deserve better. So make sure that you establish a sensible cash reserve before you start plowing money into long-term investments like real estate or 401 Ks. And when in doubt, keep more cash on hand than you think you need.

8. Have a Budget and a Plan

The plans of the diligent certainly lead to profit, but anyone who is reckless only becomes poor.

Proverbs 21:5 HCSB

You need a written monthly budget that tells you how much cash is supposed to come in and where it's supposed to go. If you don't have a budget, or if your budget is woefully out of date, the proper time to draft one is immediately (which means before you lay your head on the pillow tonight).

9. Since Money Can't Buy Happiness, Simplify

A simple life in the Fear-of-God is better than a rich life with a ton of headaches.

Proverbs 15:16 MSG

If your material possessions are somehow distancing you from God, discard them. And if you'd like to experience peace and happiness, don't expect money to buy it for you. Sure, you need the basic necessities of life, but once you've met those needs for yourself and your family, the piling up of possessions may create more problems than it solves. When in doubt, simplify.

10. Focus Not on What Your Neighbors Have, But on What You Need

Do not covet your neighbor's house . . . or anything that belongs to your neighbor.

Exodus 20:17 HCSB

When you watch your neighbors pull out their credit cards in order to buy more and more stuff, it's normal to want to keep up with the Joneses. But keeping up with high-spending neighbors is both foolish and futile. So don't do it.

11. You Live in a Society that Runs on—and May Eventually Be Consumed by—Debt. But You Must Not Allow Debt to Consume You.

The borrower is servant to the lender.

Proverbs 22:7 NLT

Just because society is consumed by debt doesn't mean that you should be. So unless you're using affordable amounts of debt to acquire an asset that is likely to go up (like the home you live in), don't borrow money. Why? Because using debt to acquire things that go down in value is slow-motion financial suicide, that's why!

12. Don't Use Credit Cards Unless You Can Pay Off the Balance Every Month

Don't run up debts, except for the huge debt of love you owe each other.

Romans 13:8 MSG

If you use your credit card to purchase consumer items, and if you pay the balance on your card off *every month*, you're probably okay. After all, carrying a credit card is usually safer than hauling around large amounts of cash, plus the credit card company gives you a written record of what you've spent.

But if you overspend, or if you can't pay off your credit card balance *every month*, you'll soon find yourself paying absurd amounts of interest. So if you can use credit cards responsibly, use them; if you can't, pay them off, cut them up, and pay cash.

13. Remember That Debt Has Both a Monetary and a Psychological Cost

Worry is a heavy load . . . .

Proverbs 12:25 NCV

Debt weighs upon both the pocketbook and the mind. And excessive debt weighs upon the mind excessively. So remember that the cost of a loan is not only the interest you pay, but also the peace-of-mind that you forfeit.

14. Be Willing to Make the Sacrifices—and Be Willing to Do the Hard Work—Required to Own Your Home Free and Clear of Debt

Wealth gotten by vanity shall be diminished: but he that gathereth by labor shall increase.

Proverbs 13:11 KJV

Ask people who have paid off their home mortgages, and they'll tell you it's a very good feeling *not* to plunk down a mortgage payment every month. Of course, owning a smaller home free-and-clear isn't the flashy way to manage your finances, but sometimes the old-fashioned ways are best.

So before you decide to take out a bigger loan and move to a bigger home, pay off—or at the very least, make a substantial dent in—the mortgage on your current abode. It's the peaceful way to own a home.

15. Vow to Invest Only in Things You Really Understand

Wisdom is the principal thing; therefore get wisdom: and with all thy getting get understanding.

Proverbs 4:7 KJV

Far too many investors—including amateur investors who don't know better and professional money managers who should know better—charge ahead with far too much fervor and far too little understanding. And they get themselves in trouble. So don't put your money into overly sophisticated investments that you can't really figure out from the prospectus. If you can't understand it, don't own it.

And the same goes for the general makeup of your investment portfolio. Don't depend upon anyone else to understand the allocation of your personal resources. Don't turn those decisions over to your broker, to your banker, to your butcher, to your baker, or to your candlestick maker. Know precisely what you're investing in before you invest. And if the investment is too complicated for you to understand in a reasonable amount of time, don't make it.

16. Don't Expect to Get Rich Quickly and Don't Expect Something for Nothing

Forsake foolishness and live, and go in the way of understanding.

Proverbs 9:6 NKJV

Avoid pie-in-the-sky investments, penny stocks, get-rich-quick schemes, and pyramid investment strategies; they're designed, not to *make* you money, but to *take* your money.

So when you're investing, think long-term, not lotto.

17. Keep Your Investments Diversified

Be sure to stay busy and plant a variety of crops, for you never know which will grow—perhaps they all will.

Ecclesiastes 11:6 NLT

Once you begin investing, stay diversified. Savvy investors understand that it's unwise to keep all one's eggs in a single basket. So stay diversified.

18. Remember That Lost Time Is Also a Major Risk That You Can and Should Manage

Hard work means prosperity; only fools idle away their time.

Proverbs 12:11 NLT

Your time is more valuable than you think, and if you don't handle it with care, you're likely to waste it. But because you live in a society that has perfected the art of time-squandering (think video games and reality TV), you'll be tempted to waste more time than you save.

So if you don't yet have the career or the net worth you desire, increase the amount of time you invest in continuing education. And while you're at it, please don't waste hours in front of the television screen. Your time is more valuable than that, and so is your future.

19. Don't Co-sign Somebody Else's Note

My child, if you co-sign a loan for a friend or guarantee the debt of someone you hardly know—if you have trapped yourself by your agreement and are caught by what you said—quick, get out of it if you possibly can! You have placed yourself at your friend's mercy.

Proverbs 6:1-3 NLT

The above Bible verse says it all.

20. Be Generous

Freely you have received, freely give.

Matthew 10:8 NKJV

The Lord unfailingly dispenses more gifts to philanthropists than to skinflints, so do the right thing by sharing what you have. When in doubt, be more generous than necessary. And then get ready for the spiritual, emotional, and material blessings that accrue to people like you who give more than they take from life.